The wealthy shipowner Sir William Burrell was one o.
art collectors who rediscovered seventeenth-century embroid_____
early years of this century. Attracted by its technical brilliance and
naïve charm he amassed a large collection ranging from embroidered
cushions and bed hangings to costume accessories and ceremonial
items. The bold images of canvas work pictures (of which there are
more than 30 examples in the Collection) were of particular interest to
him. They are full of intriguing detail and their designs are drawn from
a diversity of sources including herbals, emblem and pattern books and
illustrated bibles. Many were produced by professional draughtsmen
and sold with the required materials, as the first embroidery kits.

Professionals and amateurs alike produced highly accomplished
work, and the way in which the technical skill developed through the
making of samplers and caskets is discussed by the author. The embroidery is also examined in its social and historical context which high-
lights the underlying significance of the work. In particular, the political meaning of several pieces worked during the troubled period of the
1640s and 50s is revealed for the first time.

For conservation reasons only a few of the embroideries are on
display at one time and so this book with over 80 illustrations in full
colour brings an outstanding, yet relatively unknown collection to a
wider public.

Liz Arthur is trained as a textile conservator and since 1984 has
been curator of Glasgow Museums' large and important textile collections. She has published widely and has contributed a chapter to
Boudin at Trouville by Vivien Hamilton. She has also edited *Keeping
Glasgow in Stitches,* published by Mainstream.

EMBROIDERY 1600 – 1700

AT THE BURRELL COLLECTION

Liz Arthur

◆

EMBROIDERY
1600 – 1700
AT THE BURRELL
COLLECTION

John Murray

IN ASSOCIATION WITH

Glasgow Museums

1995

© Glasgow Museums 1995

First published 1995
by John Murray (Publishers) Ltd
50 Albemarle Street, London W1X 4BD
in association with Glasgow Museums

Exhibition: The Needle's Prayse
The Burrell Collection, Pollok Country Park, Glasgow
23 February to 14 May 1995

ISBN 0 7195 5413 6

Designed by Peter Campbell

Printed and bound in Great Britain by Butler & Tanner Ltd, Frome and London

CONTENTS

FOREWORD

SIR WILLIAM BURRELL's embroidery collection is less well known than his tapestries or carpets, but it deserves recognition for its consistently high quality. Just as other arts reflect the culture and history of the time, so too a study of embroideries can give us an insight into the lives and attitudes of their makers. This insight also enhances our enjoyment and appreciation of their work. Since the early 20th century there has been an interest in the embroidery of the early modern period which has increased markedly in recent years. This book and the accompanying exhibition are Glasgow Museums' response to that interest and to public demand for more information about the many fascinating items in the Burrell Collection.

I would like first of all to thank my colleague, Liz Arthur, who has researched and written this book and organised the exhibition. They are a tribute to her knowledge, dedication and skill and, I am sure, will give pleasure to a great many people. Thanks are also due to the following for their help in the preparation of this book: the Earl of Haddington and Mrs Flora Turnbull, Curator of Mellerstain House; the Trustees and staff of the National Library of Scotland; the Librarian of Glasgow University Library and the staff of the Special Collections; the staff of the Royal Museum of Scotland; the staff of the Holburne Museum and Craft Study Centre, Bath; Jo-Ann Gloger, Forge Mill Needle Museum; the staff of the Colonial Williamsburg Foundation; and the Countess Haig. Particular thanks must go to Mrs Margaret Swain; Ann French and the staff of Glasgow Museums, especially Ina Graham, Patricia Bascom, Patricia Collins, Vivien Hamilton, Carol Maconachie and Lynn Dalgleish. It has been our pleasure to co-operate once again with John Murray Publishers and we extend our thanks to their staff.

JULIAN SPALDING
Director, Glasgow Museums

EMBROIDERY 1600 – 1700

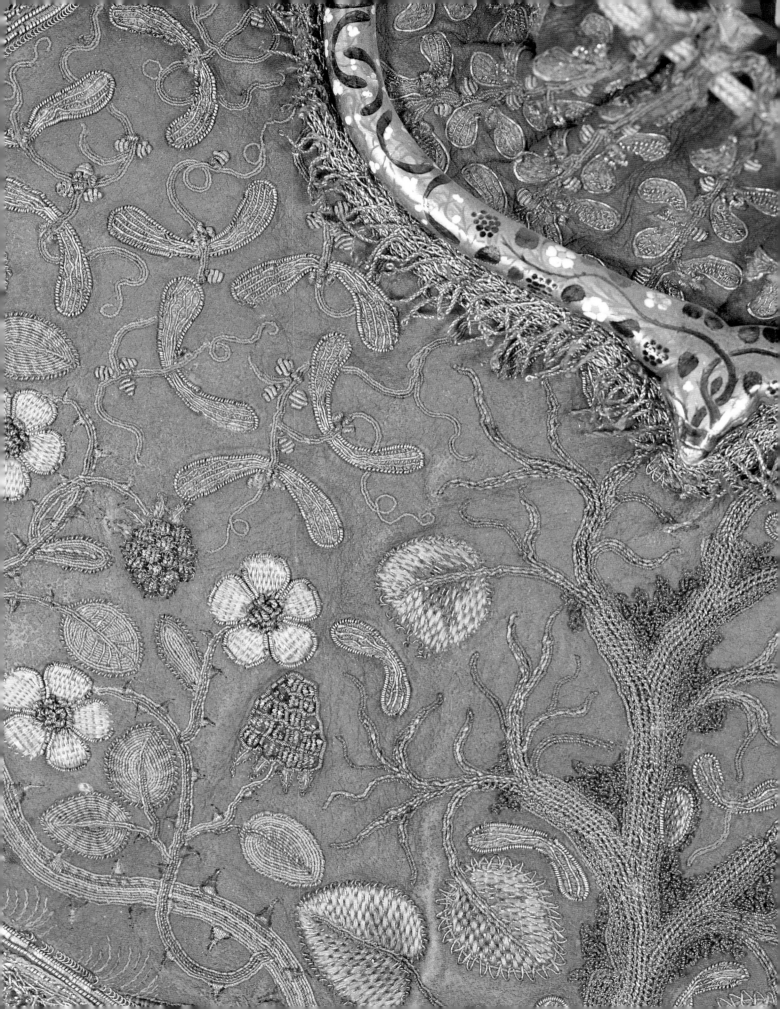

THE WEALTHY SHIPOWNER Sir William Burrell (1861–1958) was devoted to art collecting. He amassed a collection of approximately 6,000 items which were gifted to Glasgow in 1944 and added a further 2,000 items during the following thirteen years. Burrell was a very astute collector and succeeded in forming major collections in almost all his areas of interest. These included needlework and lace of high quality dating from the 14th to the 19th century. There are 121 pieces of lace; sixteen colourful examples of Ottoman and Uzbekistan embroidery; sixteen monochrome pieces from the Greek Islands and 310 other embroideries, most of which are British. The largest group of embroideries dates from the late 16th to the early 18th century and consists of embroidered garments such as jackets, women's and men's caps, boxes, caskets, mirror frames, seat covers and bed hangings. Most of all Burrell was attracted to the small canvas work pictures of which there are thirty-one. The embroideries can be admired not only as decorative objects in their own right but also for the remarkable skill involved in creating them. They are also often full of symbolism and layers of meaning, reflecting the times in which they were made. This is particularly true of the 17th-century embroideries which are most comprehensively represented in the Collection. The aim of this book is to illustrate these and set them in their historical and social context. The illustrations are all of works in the Burrell Collection, except the design sources which are credited individually and the charger from the Colonial Williamsburg Collection. Publications referred to in the text are listed on pages 122–4.

It is not known when Burrell began collecting 17th-century embroidery, but it was certainly before 1901 when his loan to the International Exhibition in Glasgow included an

1. DETAIL OF HAWKING POUCH [PL.4]

Leather embroidered with silver wire and thread of flat, thinly beaten silver wound round a silk core in chain stitch and bullion knots with strips of flat silver. The bramble stems consist of parallel rows of silk threads couched with silver and the cords and tassels are exquisitely made of silks and metal threads. The pouch is lined with silk. (29/151)

13

2. TOWER SITTING ROOM, HUTTON CASTLE, 1940S OR 50S
On the window wall is a long cushion [pl. 15], on the right the finding of Moses [pl. 66], then an 18th-century
embroidery and on the far right a raised work panel [pl. 43].

embroidered panel of 'Charles I and his Queen'. However, we do know that this interest was part of his general appreciation of the decorative arts of the 16th and 17th centuries, a period during which domestic embroidery was at its height.

Burrell's interest in Elizabethan and Jacobean furnishings was part of a widespread fascination at that time with the style of a period when the arts in Britain flourished. The fusion of Renaissance ideas and Gothic forms had created an extravagantly decorative and distinctly English style. Perhaps not surprisingly this early 20th-century nostalgia was particularly evident in the aftermath of the First World War when the country looked inwards in an attempt to come to terms with a totally changed world order. There was an affinity with the 17th century, which had also been a time of fundamental change and creative energy.

14

3. TOWER SITTING ROOM, HUTTON CASTLE, 1940S OR 50S
Above the fireplace is one of the Campbell of Glenorchy valances *c.* 1550 (29/181) and a late 17th-century
stomacher (29/147). On the left is an embroidered mirror frame (29/226).

The interest in historical embroidery was encouraged by the Arts and Crafts Movement towards the end of the 19th century. An understanding of the best embroidery from the past was seen as a means of improving the standard of contemporary design and public taste. This was one of the ideas which underpinned the embroidery department at the Glasgow School of Art and which gave rise to a major exhibition held there in 1916 to raise funds for the British Red Cross Society and other war charities. Among the distinguished members co-opted on to the organising committee were Phoebe Traquair, May Morris, Sir Robert Lorimer and of course the founders of the embroidery department at the school, Jessie Newbery and Ann Macbeth.

Burrell lent fourteen embroideries and various chairs with needlework upholstery. These

15

items must have been bought before 1911 as he made no record of them in his purchase books which begin in that year. The exhibition consisted of over one thousand items loaned by museums such as the Victoria and Albert Museum, London, the Art Gallery and Museum, Birmingham, and the Bowes Museum, Barnard Castle, by art schools in Edinburgh, Aberdeen and Dublin, as well as by individuals. Major collectors such as Sir William and Lady Lawrence and Robert Spence (whose collection of gloves is now in Bath Museum of Costume) also lent large groups of exhibits. It is significant that one of the largest loans, of forty embroidered items, was not from Burrell but from John Holms of Formakin, Bishopton. Like Burrell, Holms was a successful local businessman (a stockbroker) who arguably amassed an even greater fine and decorative art collection than Burrell. Unlike Burrell, however, he had to sell it.

The interest in embroidery was encouraged by people like Lilla Hailstone of Horton Hall who published an illustrated catalogue of her collection, *Ancient Framed Needlework Pictures*, in 1897. Dealers were quick to promote a new area of collecting and in 1900 the Fine Art Society, London, organised an exhibition in which 350 samplers, embroidered pictures and other decorative pieces were shown. At this time there were few serious collectors of needlework but it fitted the current general area of interest and was encouraged by writers such as Marcus Huish, editor of *The Art Journal*, and Mrs Rachel Head, herself a collector, who wrote articles for *Connoisseur* magazine, launched in 1901. This increased interest brought important collections on to the market, such as Viscountess Wolseley's Stuart needlework which was sold in 1906. Although Burrell owned a few pieces by this date, it is not known how many. However he was not renowned for being at the forefront of collecting, and as he reflected trends rather than shaped them, it is probable that he owned only a few at this time. It was only after 1916 that he built up the main part of his Collection.

There were other collectors like himself and John Holms, highly successful businessmen, such as Lord Lever, who bought embroideries of the highest quality and whose collections have been preserved. Just as Burrell was able to take advantage of the dispersal of John Holms' collection and to buy stained glass and architectural stonework from Randolph Hearst, so too he was able to acquire important embroideries from the collections of Percival Griffiths and Frank Ward. The key to his acquisitions was his appreciation of quality and craftsmanship, and these are central to the whole Collection, whether in European and Asian decorative arts or in artefacts from ancient civilisations.

Burrell's main collecting years were 1916, when he bought thirteen embroideries, and 1917, when he bought twenty-seven. This followed his purchase of Hutton Castle, near Berwick-upon-Tweed, in 1916, although he and Lady Burrell did not move in until 1927

4. POUCH FROM THE HAWKING ACCOUTREMENTS, EARLY 17TH CENTURY
The set includes a gauntlet, lure, two hoods, whistle, vervels, hobble and bells. The pouch would have been
suspended from a belt and is like a double bag with two identical embroidered sections joined by a
hinge below the loop. 37 cm × 44 cm (29/151).

when most of the extensive refurbishment work had been done [pls 2, 3]. However, the
installation of panelling and stained glass was not complete until 1929. He continued to buy
steadily, adding between two and eleven pieces each year from 1918 until 1947. Unfortunately
no correspondence relating to these purchases survives.

He recorded his purchases methodically in lined exercise books, noting the date, the cost, from whom purchased and the date of delivery. These give an invaluable insight into his pattern of collecting. Although it is well known that he prized his tapestries highly and was often prepared to pay more for them than for paintings, his interest in, and the importance of, his embroidery has been overshadowed by other areas of the Collection. In 1918, at a time when his collecting focused on painting, 15 per cent of his expenditure was on needlework to be enjoyed for its decorative and artistic qualities. This 15 per cent does not include furniture with needlework upholstery, such as settees, firescreens or bed hangings intended for everyday use at Hutton Castle.

Although the purchase books are very useful, his descriptions are often frustratingly vague. The terms 'stump picture', 'fine old Stuart petit point picture' and 'sampler' appear all too frequently making it difficult to identify many items with any accuracy. Even more tantalising are brief references to items sold and to entries such as that for 16 April 1917 for a 'Needlework Susanna and the Elders', but to which of the two pictures of this subject this refers remains a mystery. This makes it very difficult to check the provenance of the pieces.

Burrell bought from many people, including some of the major stores such as Debenham and Freebody, London, Jenner and Co., Edinburgh, and Wylie and Lochhead, Glasgow, who were all catering for the public taste in things 'Jacobethan'. Over the years Burrell consistently dealt with the London dealers John Hunt, Frank Partridge and Acton Surgey, from whom he also bought furniture, ceramics, tapestries and stained glass. It was from Partridge in 1934 that he bought four important items from the Percival Griffiths collection. These included the set of hawking accoutrements said to have belonged to James VI and I for which he paid £1,100 [pls 1, 4].

Burrell is known to have been a canny buyer and although embroidery was not a major collecting area he was prepared to spend this considerable sum which was more than he paid for many of his smaller tapestries. Comparing this amount (which would have bought a sizeable detached house at that time) with other expenditure gives an idea of how highly both Burrell and the market valued this piece. For example, in the following year a late 15th-century chasuble with Opus Anglicanum embroidery was priced at £405; a Charles II silver candlestick £60; in 1933 a pastel by Degas cost him £360 and in 1935 a Raeburn portrait £600.

The hawking set of accoutrements is of the highest quality of craftsmanship. The leather is embroidered with blackberries and mistletoe. The blackberry was known as the 'blessed bramble' in the Scottish highlands because of its healing properties and it was twined with ivy and rowan to ward off witches and evil spirits. As anyone who has gone brambling knows, the most luscious fruits just out of reach can be a snare, and it may be this idea which was intended as the blackberry is paired with the mistletoe, a symbol of life and a protective talisman. The mounts are of enamelled gold believed by Burrell to be the work of George Heriot, jeweller to James VI, but apart from the quality of the work there is no evidence to prove this. The set is possibly Scottish (there were professional embroiderers working in Edinburgh in the 16th and 17th centuries) but it could also perhaps be French. Other hawking sets of this period are less opulent. One, which belonged to King Christian IV of Denmark, was simpler, as is a pouch carried by Sir Thomas Gresham that can be seen in a late 16th-century portrait now in the National Portrait Gallery, London.

The appeal of the hawking set was not only the exquisite quality but also the historical associations which lend weight to the claims for its origins. It was said to have been left at Wroxton Abbey, Oxfordshire, by King James when he visited on 23 August 1619. This visit can be reasonably substantiated by a letter which confirmed that he was entertained 'with the fashionable and courtly diversions of hawking and bear baiting'.[1] Although the sport was going out of fashion the king was a notable falconer and there are several portraits of him as a child with a hawk. A royal visit caused great expense for the host, but it was a real mark of favour and the occasion was commemorated with a stained and painted window which would have been relatively simple to organise as workmen were busy rebuilding part of the house at the time of the visit. The window is now in the Royal Museum of Scotland, Edinburgh. It is unlikely that the hawking set was given to Lord Dudley North (d. 1677), as Burrell believed, because Wroxton was owned by Sir William Pope (1573–1631) at the time of the visit. It was only later, in 1680, that it came into the North family when Francis North bought over the estate from the family of his wife, Frances Pope.

Burrell was very interested in heraldry in every medium. One of the most detailed entries for a textile purchase is that of 25 August 1938 in which he describes all the complex quarterings of a linen panel woven with the arms of Anne of Denmark in 1603. He also liked pieces purported to have belonged to historically important individuals. Accordingly such items have longer descriptions in the purchase books. For example, in 1937 he bought a cap, tunic and shoes said to have been worn in 1645 by Charles II when Prince of Wales and also a cap, gloves and two combs formerly owned by Oliver Cromwell. Perhaps he accepted these claims too readily and without evidence, but the embroideries are certainly fine pieces.

Although most of the Collection was kept at Hutton Castle some of the embroideries were lent to museums such as the Bowes Museum at Barnard Castle, Luton Museum and the Art Gallery at Torquay while many more were lent to exhibitions throughout the country. He also gave a small collection of embroideries to the Bowes Museum.

CHAPTER 2

THE EMBROIDERERS

THE PROFESSIONALS

THERE ARE SEVERAL examples of embroidery made by professionals in the Collection, but none that can be attributed. Even the splendid ceremonial items are the work of anonymous embroiderers. It is known that professional workers had their own guild and that some had workshops, some were attached to aristocratic households to draw designs and supervise their execution by the ladies of the house, and some travelled the country. A medieval guild existed but it was refounded as the Broderers' Company which was granted its charter for the organisation of professional work in 1561. Little is known of these professional workers, but those working for the court must have succeeded financially as several left money to build almshouses for the poor. From inventories we have descriptions of the garments made for Queen Elizabeth by John Parr who became embroiderer to James VI and I after 1603. As well as making elaborate and impressive garments for state occasions, Parr worked small pieces such as caps and edgings for shoes. In 1594 he embroidered a lawn coif (woman's cap) 'richly worked' with black silk and gold and another with black silk and silver.[2] The extensive use of precious metal threads made these pieces valuable. Professional workers also repaired embroideries by cutting out the worked areas and transferring them to new fabric or another garment.

One of the most important members of the Broderers' guild was Edmund Harrison (1589–1666), Court Embroiderer to James VI and I, Charles I and Charles II. He was Warden of the Broderers' Company and embroidered masque costumes for the court and

5. LORD CHANCELLOR'S BURSE, 1682
Made for Francis North, Baron Guilford. None of the velvet ground has been left undecorated.
It is sumptuously worked with silver and silver-gilt threads, purls and spangles as befits the status of the office.
43 cm × 40.5 cm (29/153).

liveries for court officials. He was paid £12.17.6 (£12.75) for embroidering the binding of the Red Book of the Order of the Garter.[3]

Many of the workshops would produce large wall coverings, tents, horse furniture, table carpets and ceremonial furnishings. The Collection contains two splendid examples: the 16th-century Luttrell table carpet and the Kimberley throne which was purchased by Burrell in 1947. This composite piece was made for the great hall at Kimberley for Queen Elizabeth when she made her tour of the eastern counties in 1578. It is embroidered with the arms of Woodehouse and Corbet.

Workshops also produced heralds' tabards and other items embroidered with impressive coats of arms such as the burse for the Great Seal bought by Burrell in 1948 from Acton Surgey [pl. 5]. This was made for Francis North (1637–85), Baron Guilford, who was appointed Lord Chancellor, Keeper of the Great Seal, by Charles II in 1682. The individual motifs of the arms of Charles II were worked separately on linen-covered card, padded with heavy cords and the surface covered by coarse canvas. Silver and silver-gilt threads were then couched on top. Finally the back had paper pasted over it to prevent fraying before the motif was secured to the red velvet ground with slip stitches, and the edges covered by silver-gilt wire. The central arms were worked on heavy canvas which has been bent under and stitched at intervals. It was probably stiffened with glue to allow it to remain proud of the surface, the effect being similar to carved and undercut woodwork. The red velvet has then been sprinkled with sequins held in place with bullion knots. The back of the bag has been left plain as this would not show when it was being carried. The silk tassels are made on a solid shape which has been covered in pink and red silk threads with metal threads worked over the top. The weighty, dignified effect befits the grandeur and importance of the office. Ceremonial items did not change during the 17th century and the company established by the Shudall family in the Temple Bar, London (the centre of the tailoring trade where there were many other trades including embroiderers), continues (under the name Ede and Ravenscroft) to make ceremonial garments embellished with rich embroidery.

Although there are references to professional embroiderers in wills and records of the Broderers' Company, few examples of their work can be attributed to specific workers. An exception is the set of signed and dated panels completed in 1637 by Edmund Harrison who was commissioned by Sir William Howard to work them with scenes from the life of the Virgin Mary (two are in the Royal Museum of Scotland, Edinburgh, one in the Victoria and Albert Museum, London, and one in the Fitzwilliam Museum, Cambridge). From these it is obvious that the figures and the compositions were more sophisticated than those worked by amateurs. Professional embroiderers worked all the figures separately and then applied

6. CAP AND SLIPPERS, *c.* 1640–80
Silk embroidered with loops of silver and silver-gilt thread and spangles.
(29/133, 144, 145).

them to the fabric. Sometimes they were padded to give extra depth to the composition but the three-dimensional appearance of the figures was created by careful use of shading and perspective akin to needle painting. The techniques used by professionals continued the medieval tradition of split stitch for faces and hands and *or nué*, in which gold embroidery thread was couched down with coloured silks. It was possible to create subtle effects by laying the couching threads close together. Neither of these techniques was widely used by

23

amateurs. Literature contains few references to professional embroiderers but in an anonymous play, *Sir Giles Goosecap* published in 1606, there is a lighthearted reference to their skill:

> He will work you any flower to the life, as like delicate
> perfumer, he will give it you his perfect and natural
> savour . . . He will make you flies and worms of all sorts,
> most lively, and is now working on a whole bed embroidered
> with nothing but glow worms whose light, has so perfectly
> that you may go to bed in the chamber . . . without a candle.

The high standards of secular embroidery established in the 16th century continued under the Stuart kings James and his son Charles I, who was a great patron of the arts. However, Charles's unpopular policies and increasing difficulties with Parliament throughout the 1630s brought about political unrest. This affected the demand for embroidery and in 1634 a

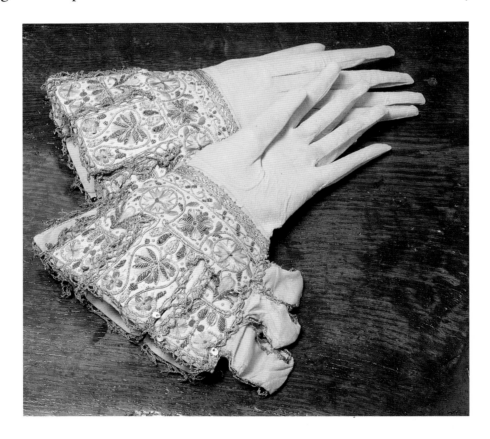

7. GLOVES, *c.* 1600–30
Leather with silk and metal thread embroidery. Gloves were given as formal gifts and were often
displayed by being carried or worn in the belt. (29/141).

petition from the Broderers' Company to the king states that 'The trade is now so much decayed and grown out of use, so that a great part of the Company for want of employment are so much impoverished as they are constrained to become porters, watercarriers and the like.'⁴ The Civil War and eventual execution of the king made matters worse. With the exile of the court and the establishment of the Commonwealth under Cromwell as Lord Protector, there was even less pageantry and ceremony. In religious matters the Puritans were committed to the Reformation and so favoured plain unadorned interiors with none of the lavishly embroidered altar vestments used formerly.

Although masques continued, they were not as lavish and professional embroiderers fell on very hard times. In 1660, after the Restoration, their fortunes revived and Edmund Harrison petitioned Charles II for arrears due to him for embroidering 250 coats of the Yeomen of the Chamber and a cloth of estate and a carpet belonging to Charles I which he had hidden and returned to the new monarch.⁵

There was still some secular embroidery worked during the Commonwealth. Items of clothing such as the quilted tunic and embroidered cap and slippers bought by Burrell in 1937 were still being made [pl. 6]. These were said to have been worn by Charles II as Prince of Wales in 1645 while staying in the house of Sir Thomas Veal of Alverstone, near Bristol, when he was sent to take charge of the Royalist forces in the west of England. They were sold to Frank Partridge and Sons by a direct descendant of the family and although the embroidery is probably professional work the provenance is unsubstantiated.

Gloves with elaborately embroidered cuffs were a mark of rank and often given as gifts and tokens of fidelity. This was a continuation of the medieval practice of a lady giving her glove to her knight who then wore it fastened to his helmet. A painting by Nicholas Hilliard of George Clifford, Earl of Cumberland, shows him as the Knight of Pendragon Castle and Queen's Champion with the Queen's glove set in the front of his cap (National Maritime Museum, London). Decorated gloves were also worn for the obvious practical purpose of keeping the hands warm and clean while travelling. They were often perfumed with jasmine oil, cumin, cloves, nutmeg or rosewater.

Burrell bought two pairs of gloves. Those said to have belonged to Oliver Cromwell have small gauntlets embroidered in brightly coloured silks with tulips and rather crudely drawn birds. There are also spangles and a silver fringed edging. The other more magnificent pair has much larger richly worked gauntlet cuffs, trimmed with silver lace [pl. 7].

Other small items such as the tiny bags decorated with flowers, which may have been given as gifts, sometimes containing money or trinkets, would have been produced in the workshops. These bags may also have been intended as 'swete bages', filled with sweet-

8. (LEFT) SWEET BAG, *c.* 1600–30
Silk and metal threads with silver tassels. Apart from the exquisite embroidery, the making of the cords and tassels
was an art form in itself and books of instructions explaining the technique were published.
10 cm × 10.5 cm (excluding tassels) (29/310).

9. (RIGHT) DETAIL OF SAMPLER, MID 17TH CENTURY
Linen worked with silks, silver and silver-gilt threads in tent and buttonhole stitches with raised and padded work.
The roses are set in a formal framework in imitation of the popular knot gardens of the period. See also plate 82.
52.7 cm × 26 cm (31/6).

smelling herbs such as lavender, to put in with linen and clothes stored in chests [pl. 8]. They
were also carried suspended from the waist and many surviving bags have tiny pin-cushions
attached. Designs have been found on samplers of the same date which suggests that the bags
may also have been worked by amateurs [pl. 9].

It is often impossible to differentiate between professional and amateur work. In many
cases amateur work was more carefully finished and finely executed than that of the professional, especially the small items for personal or domestic use. However, items which would
have been difficult to stitch because of the nature of the material were probably professional

work. For example the fine chain stitching on the hawking accoutrements would not have been within the capacity of an amateur because the leather was difficult to work.

Embroidery was a necessary skill for young women and some of the professional embroiderers turned to supplying the increasing number of amateurs with ready-drawn patterns and equipment, the first embroidery kits. At the beginning of the 20th century, when Burrell began his collection, it was thought that 17th-century embroideresses produced their own designs which were regarded as charming and quaint, but this has been shown not to be the case. The number of similar embroideries based on the same themes points to the existence of professional draughtsmen producing multiple copies for sale. Also, the likelihood of amateurs combining the same flowers and insects with the same story, in the same arrangement, is remote. For example, two embroideries in the Burrell Collection depicting

10. JOSEPH FLEEING FROM POTIPHAR'S WIFE, *c.* 1630–50
Linen with silk threads in canvas work. Potiphar's wife is shown as was usual with her skirt brazenly pulled above her knee to reveal her smock and show her lascivious intentions. One of two almost identical pictures in the Collection; a third shows the scene reversed. 22 cm × 32 cm (29/54).

II. DESIGN FOR EMBROIDERY, MID 17TH CENTURY

Some of the motifs are outlined in black silk tent stitch. On the left of this rural landscape is the disobedient prophet, who has been thrown from his ass and killed by a lion. In the corners of the border are the personifications of the elements: Air holding a chameleon, Fire with a torch, Water, a trident and Earth with fruit. A worked version of the central design is in a private collection.
46.6 cm × 55 cm (29/102).

12. ILLUSTRATION BY BERNARD SALOMON, 1553

This illustration was probably the source for the design of the disobedient prophet [pl. 11]. From *The True and Lyvely Historyke Purtreatures of the Vvoll Bible*, published by Jean de Tours in Lyons, 1553. Courtesy of the Trustees of the National Library of Scotland.

Joseph spurning the advances of his master Potiphar's wife [pl. 10] are virtually identical to one in the Lady Lever Gallery, Liverpool. These designs were derived from woodcuts and engravings, and although the needlewoman could have copied them herself, the original engravings are small and would have needed to be enlarged [pls 11, 12]. The existence of professional draughtsmen who could adapt printed designs to their customers' needs may also explain why so few embroideries can be directly attributed to designs in pattern books.

There are often small areas of embroideries left unfinished, where the young embroideress has tired of the piece, and sometimes the silk threads have worn away to expose the original drawing underneath. The fine quality of these ink drawings is further proof of their

13. DESIGN FOR EMBROIDERY, MID 17TH CENTURY
Drawn on satin with some motifs worked in split stitch and others worked separately and applied. The caterpillar and stems of the flowers are of couched threads and cords. The central figure may be Samson or Hercules and derives from emblem books where the figure represents Magnanimity. On either side are personifications of Hearing and Sight and below, the elephant represents Africa and the horse either Europe or Time.
37.5 cm × 54 cm (29/311).

source. An elaborate, unfinished panel bought from the Royal School of Needlework, London, in 1921 is convincing evidence not only of the hand of a professional draughtsman, but also of Burrell's serious interest in needlework [pls 11, 12].

The draughtsman would use a fine quill pen to draw the outline of the design in black ink on either fine linen canvas or thick white silk satin. Sometimes watercolour was used to indicate shading and facial features. Such assured control of ink and watercolour on absorbent textiles would have been almost impossible for the amateur to achieve [pl. 13].

Of the few surviving embroideries which can be attributed to particular designers one is in Blair Castle, Perthshire. The panel of unknown subject is signed in ink 'Jo. Nelham Sugar Lofe Grayffriars Newgate Market'. Research has shown that John Nelham and his father Roger were embroidery designers from the 1630s until the 1680s. In 1654 Roger Nelham's will stated that he left 'half of my books and prints and patterns which I do use for the drawing of works ... all my beams and lathes and working instruments ... which do appertain and belong to my work house' to his elder son John, and the other half to his younger son Samuel.[6]

Burrell's design has recently been discovered to have the initial M written in the border at the top and bottom, and there is an inscription along the hem at the bottom right, in faded ink. Unfortunately the inscription has been badly damaged by the nail holes which secured the canvas to the frame and it has not yet been deciphered. It is hoped that in due course it will be and the identity of the draughtsman revealed which will add to our scant knowledge of these professional workers.

14. DETAIL OF BLACKWORK, EARLY 17TH CENTURY
This 7 cm-wide embroidery is worked along two sides of each of a pair of pillow cases. 48 cm × 95 cm (29/235).

It was not only the professionals who were technically proficient; the amateurs who produced most of the surviving work from the 17th century were also highly skilled. Amateurs were responsible for a large amount of the domestic embroidery of the period. This was the result of growth in both the wealth and numbers of the gentry after the war with Spain when trade and industry were expanding and colonisation was beginning. The gentry as a class came between the aristocracy and the yeomanry and tenant farmers. By the end of the 17th century they accounted for about 1 per cent of the total population of England of approximately seven million. The possession of land became an important social distinction and three quarters of the gentry lived in the country. Their households were normally large, made up of family and servants, and they usually had close connections with London, either political or commercial. In London they would see the latest styles and imports and be able to send descriptions home by letter and later return with samples. It is from the houses of the gentry that much of the existing needlework comes.

To establish and emphasise their status as gentlemen both men and their families had to be seen to be refined and live a leisured existence in elegant surroundings. Status was demonstrated in many ways. For example, in portraits (including miniatures) the lavish details of dress, accessories and surroundings were often more important than a likeness of the sitter. As the home was an important status symbol many were improved and new country houses with elegant gardens were built. Styles varied between the Italianate favoured by the Catholic court and the more homely brick-built Dutch architecture which appealed to the Protestants. Large expensive glass windows were introduced making interiors much lighter, but the furniture was still fairly dark. The walls would be either panelled or hung with tapestries and later in the century with gilt, tooled and painted leather, and, as the taste for more exotic Chinese design developed, painted wallpaper. The rooms were sparsely furnished but the substantial wooden chairs were made more comfortable with cushions. Early in the century, as in the Middle Ages, the gentry and aristocracy often owned many houses and moved from one to another. They took their furnishings with them and these tapestries, bed hangings, table carpets, cushions and linen were their status symbols. By the 1690s, as people became more settled, there was less need to have easily transportable furnishings, and more comfortable chairs and settees with upholstered seats, backs and arms were introduced. This development reflects the enormous changes during the 17th century which saw the move from a medieval society towards our modern world.

Burrell emulated the more austere style of furnishing in his own dining room which was lined with carved linenfold panelling of *c.* 1500 and furnished with oak armchairs of the late 16th and early 17th century but made more comfortable with modern red velvet cushions. He did collect some embroidered and woven velvet cushions and these were used in the hall and drawing rooms.

A Hamilton Palace inventory (now in the Hamilton Archives at Lennoxlove) for 1607 records: 'two auld pictured cuscheons', 'foure new sewit cuscheons with pictures', four sewn with 'Janetflour work', two with 'the work of the wyneberrie tree' and two 'with the roise of Calise'.[7] The interest in family status is demonstrated by the most usual type which had armorial shields enclosed in wreaths of flowers. The cushions would be for chairs or long benches and window seats. Long cushions went out of fashion in the 1630s but those for chairs and small cushions for pins continued to be made. The embroidered cushions in the Collection include one with the arms of Brabant, one with Orpheus charming the animals and one depicting the Bible story of Rebecca at the well.

Of the upholstered furniture collected and used by Burrell several pieces have interesting needlework covers [pl. 16]. Most are from the early 18th century but there are several interesting late 17th-century examples. The covers were worked in wools on canvas which was practical and hard wearing. The designs were mainly ramping flowers and foliage although there is one settee in the drawing room which has chinoiserie figures, beasts and birds which would have been in keeping with other fashionable furniture. The making of these covers, which were often in sets, was a huge undertaking. When the covers had been completed they were mounted on appropriate stools, chairs or settees which may have been specially made to fit them.

The bed, the largest and most important piece of furniture, would have had embroidered hangings that reflected the family wealth. They were made up of two wide and two narrow curtains, often in a contrasting colour to the two sets of valances, three valances hanging around the tester (canopy) and another three for the lower part of the bed below the counterpane [pl. 17]. These were worked in silks and wools on canvas in tent stitch. Sets of valances and curtains were made both in professional workshops and by amateurs. Although

15. DETAIL OF PANEL FOR A COVER, EARLY 17TH CENTURY
The dark green satin ground, now faded and discoloured, is pinked at regular intervals. The back of the fabric was probably painted with size to prevent fraying. The motifs have been worked individually on fine canvas and applied to the satin. Some inventive techniques have been used: metal purl has been stretched and the loosely coiled metal couched down and interwoven with silk threads to create insect wings and bodies. Raised work of this period often reveals delightful details when studied closely. 42 cm × 93.5 cm (29/170).

16. WINGED ARMCHAIR WITH NEEDLEWORK UPHOLSTERY, *c.* 1690
The back is decorated with a version of Susannah and the Elders and below, Elijah feeding the ravens.
Formerly in the collection of the Earl of Lovelace. (14/191).

a major, communal undertaking for amateurs it would have been a pleasant sociable occupation for the women of the household working together.

Few if any original curtains survive because of their constant use. However, many valances survive in surprisingly good condition. There are over twenty valances of the late 16th and early 17th century in the Collection, in addition to what is probably the earliest known set of three which was worked by the household of Sir Colin Campbell of Glenorchy in the early 1550s. Burrell used some of the valances for their original purpose and a photograph taken at Hutton Castle shows a valance on a four poster bed. This valance (29/184) depicts a procession of goddesses in triumphal cars. He also used them purely for decoration: another photograph shows one of the framed Campbell valances above the fireplace in the tower sitting room [pl. 3].

Valances were made throughout northern Europe and are possibly of French origin, although many of the surviving examples are Scottish. They were worked with a wide variety of subjects ranging from biblical stories and classical virtues and vices to rural and garden scenes. Those with virtues and vices were often taken from emblem books which were popular throughout Europe. Emblem books were more widely used as a source for embroidery designs than any of the pattern books, E. Geoffrey Whitney's *A Choice of Emblems and other devices* published in 1586 being one of the most popular [pl. 18]. In it he praised English culture, government and the Protestant religion and gave the impression of an exemplary society. Like so many other pattern books it was derived from Andrea Alciati's *Emblematum Liber*, first published in Augsburg in 1531, which ran to almost 180 editions and was translated into several languages. Some emblems were based on fables or myths and contained a moral, while others conveyed a proverb or wise saying. The images were usually accompanied by a motto or poem. For example a strawberry plant entwined by a snake has the motto *Latet Anguis in Herba* (The adder lurketh privily in the grass). One of the late 16th-century valances in the Collection (29/19) is worked with five emblems and mottoes. Other emblems were used as personal badges known as *imprese* and these were also embroidered on bed hangings, particularly during the 16th century. There were many secular emblem books, but religious emblems were more numerous and more widely used in the context of embroidery.

One of Burrell's valances worked in the early 17th century has several emblems from Whitney including three women playing dice [pl. 17]. In the book the women are accompanied by the following poem:

> Three careless dames around a table playing dice
> Three careless dames amongst their wanton toies,
> Did throw the dice who first of them should die

35

And she that lost, did laugh with inward joyes
For that, she thought her term should longer be
But lo a tile upon her head did fall.
That death, with spede, this dame from dice did call.

Even so, it falls while careless times we spend:
That evil hoppes, unlooked for doe come.
But if we hope, that God some good will send
In earnest prayer, then must we not be domme
For blessings good, come sealed before our prayer
But evil things do come before we fear.

To the right of the women on the valance is a blind beggar carrying a lame but sighted man. The message conveyed by this emblem is that the rich should not despise the poor because everyone in society is interdependent.

Apart from large furnishings there were many other small items in the house which provided suitable surfaces for embroidery. For example, books had become more readily available but were precious and they were often protected within extra covers embellished with embroidery. Some books were bound with embroidered covers. Most of these were devotional works and required suitable subjects. The figures of Hope holding a bird, and Faith holding an open book and a chalice were considered appropriate. They are depicted on a small pin-cushion in the Collection which was probably originally intended as a book cover [pl. 19]. Cushions on which to lay books were also embroidered [pl. 22].

Although canvas work was the most practical form of book cover elaborate embroideries with a three-dimensional effect were also used. Biblical scenes were depicted, often enclosed within a cartouche worked in metal threads. A panel in the Collection which may have been intended as a Bible cover or the top of a box shows Abraham casting aside Hagar and Ishmael with the inscription 'Sarah unto Abraham doth complain, that Ishmael no longer should remain, an heir with her son Isaac for to be, cast out therefore ye bondswoman said she' [pl. 20]. A similar composition of embroidered figures representing Elijah and the widow covers a Bible in the Irwin Untermyer Collection in the Metropolitan Museum of Art, New York.

Making household furnishings was labour intensive and in keeping with the Protestant work ethic, which meant that embroidery was regarded as virtuous. Oliver Cromwell's wife was said to have maintained, at her own expense, six clergymen's daughters whom she constantly employed at needlework.[8] Embroidery, involving sitting with the head bowed, could also be equated with piety and was seen as a suitably quiet occupation for women as John Taylor suggested in his famous poem 'The Needle's Excellency' printed for James Boler in 1631.

17. DETAIL OF BED VALANCE, LATE 16TH
OR EARLY 17TH CENTURY

Worked in tent stitch on coarse linen, depicting three women
playing dice. 40.5 cm × 183 cm (29/101) .

18. SOURCE OF DESIGN FOR VALANCE [PL. 17]

Illustration from E G Whitney's *A Choice of Emblems*, 1586. Emblems
and allegories played an important part in literature and the decorative
arts. Designs from this book were used widely in a variety of media, for
example the painting on the ceiling at Culross Palace, Fife.
Courtesy of the Librarian, Glasgow University Library.

19. BOOK COVER MADE UP AS A PIN-CUSHION, MID 17TH CENTURY
Canvas work trimmed with silver bobbin lace and pearls. The figure on the left has a silk face and hands. She
represents Hope and the figure on the right, Faith. 15 cm × 21 cm (29/157).

> And for my countries quiet, I should like,
> That woman-kinde should use no other Pike,
> It will increase their peace, enlarge their store,
> To use their tongues less, and their needles more.

From the middle of the 17th century another increasingly popular type of decoration for domestic furnishing was crewel work. This was executed in crewel wool, a lightly twisted two-ply worsted yarn, on a linen and cotton twill woven fabric [pls 23, 24]. Polychrome crewel embroidery was the most usual, but furnishings were also worked in monochrome. A set of crewel work bed hangings consisting of curtains, pelmet, cushion and bedspread

20. ABRAHAM CASTING OUT HAGAR AND ISHMAEL, MID 17TH CENTURY
Worked with silk, metal thread, metal purl and covered purl on silk satin in long and short, back and satin stitches
with couching and detached needlepoint fillings. The faces are padded and the hands of silk-covered wood. The
garments are decorated with seed pearls and lace. 28 cm × 37 cm (29/45).

worked in shades of blue was loaned to the National Trust to furnish a 17th-century bed at
Crathes Castle for three months in 1963.

Designs of bold foliage with exotic flowers growing on a tree on a small hill, sometimes
with rabbits, deer and turbaned figures, denote a growing interest in Eastern design. With
the establishment of the Dutch and English East India Companies rare and expensive
Chinese and Japanese items such as lacquerware, ceramics, painted and embroidered cot-
tons and silks came to Britain. The trading links between East and West also led to the East
imitating Western designs. The crewel embroideries were a result of reciprocal influences
between East and West and Eastern imitations of English designs were imported into

21. PANEL WITH THREE BIBLICAL SCENES, MID 17TH CENTURY
Canvas work centre with a silk border. This panel shows the influence of the Renaissance in the use of classically inspired grotesque masks and the architectural framework for the scenes depicting the sacrifice of Isaac, Moses and the burning bush, and Susannah and the Elders. Similar devices were used on the title pages of books.
See also plate 53. 31 cm × 40 cm (29/49).

Britain. The crewel work hangings were made as bed and window curtains and although there are few dated pieces they were widely used particularly during the early 18th century. Burrell bought many of these for use as curtains and bedspreads which explains the poor condition of many of them.

Costume was also enriched with embroidery, particularly early in the 17th century when the Elizabethan tradition continued. Lavishly ornate patterns of stylised floral motifs covered bodices and informal jackets [pls 25, 26, 29]. Delicate embroidery was used on underwear as well as on caps worn by both men and women, a tradition which stretched back to medieval times.

22. CUSHION, EARLY 17TH CENTURY
Linen embroidered with flowers, fruit, birds and grasshoppers in silks, silver and
silver-gilt threads. Edged with silver bobbin lace and spangles.
56 cm × 79 cm (29/189).

The lady of the manor would have been familiar with medicinal plants as she was expected to tend the sick of the household. She would have learned their healing properties and the various remedies for lesser ailments from her mother. She would also have been familiar with herbals which proliferated in the 17th century. Among the best known was John Gerard's *The Herball or Generall Historie of Plantes* first published in 1597, but republished in a much improved and revised form in 1633. In it Gerard combined botanical and herbal knowledge with a delight in plants. Universities established physic gardens such as the one in Oxford set up in 1621 in which plants were grown for their aesthetic qualities as well as for their practical use. Exotic novelties such as the potato were being introduced from the

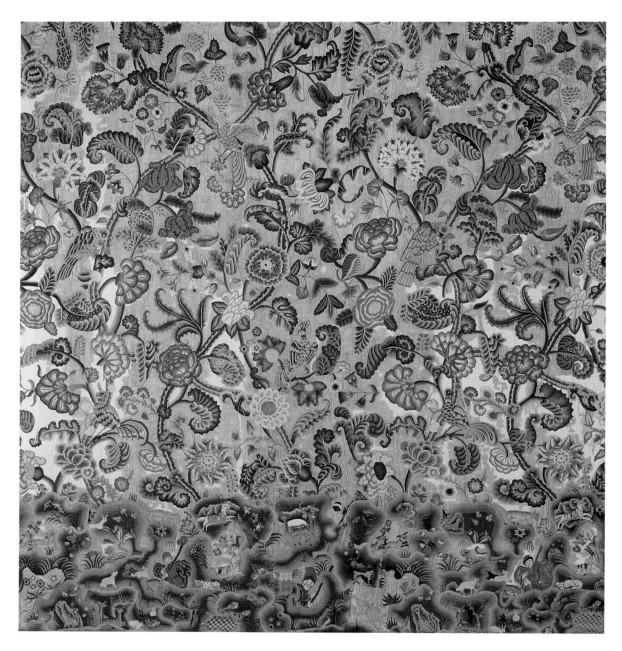

23. CURTAIN FROM A SET OF BED HANGINGS, *c.* 1690–1710

Worked with crewel wools in a variety of stitches on twill woven linen and cotton. The pattern is repeated in different colours. The parrot with cherries is from Thomas Johnson's *A Booke of Beast, Birds, Flowers, Fruits, Flies and Wormes*, published in 1630, which was still being used in the 18th century. 238 cm × 223 cm (29/241).

24. (FACING) CURTAIN FROM A SET OF BED HANGINGS, *c.* 1650–1700

Linen and cotton twill embroidered with crewel wools in stem, coral, split, long and short, and speckling stitches. 257 cm × 145 cm (29/286).

25. DETAIL OF WOMAN'S JACKET [PL. 26]

26. (FACING) WOMAN'S JACKET (BACK VIEW), *c.* 1600–25
Linen embroidered with silks, silver and silver-gilt threads in detached buttonhole, chain
and plaited braid stitches. Tightly fitted, fastening at the front and with a small collar and
epaulettes. These jackets were for semi-formal wear indoors. (29/127).

New World and nurseries were established to cater for the growing demand for unusual and
desirable cultivated plants. This was the period of Dutch tulipomania which reached its peak
in the 1630s when large sums of money were spent on new varieties of tulip. With this
background it was therefore not surprising that this new knowledge of flowers and plants
should be reflected in the embroidery of the time [pls 27, 28].

Commonly grown flowers and fruit were the most popular subjects for embroidery,
particularly roses, honeysuckle, tulips, pinks, strawberries and acorns. Some of the flowers
were cultivated in nosegay gardens during the early 17th century and many had symbolic

44

 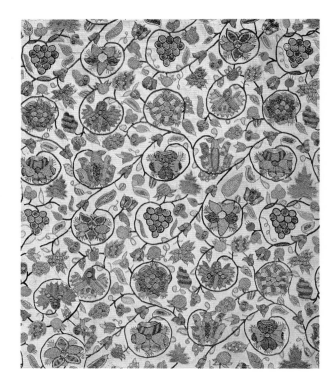

27. (LEFT) DETAIL OF CANVAS WORK PANEL, MID 17TH CENTURY
The ground is worked in rococo stitch and the raised motifs have been worked separately and applied. The plants
have been copied from herbals and are known as slips from the method of propagation which is identified by the
small spur at the base of the cutting where it has been pulled from the stem. Plants illustrated in herbals are often
drawn in this way. 29 cm × 40 cm (29/37).

28. (RIGHT) DETAIL OF PANEL, EARLY 17TH CENTURY
Linen with silk and metal threads in highly textured embroidery including plaited braid stitches. This type of
embroidery was used for both women's jackets and pillow covers, known as pillow beres. 51 cm × 41 cm (29/20).

significance, especially the rose, which was widely used. Gerard recommended the rose 'for
his beautie, virtues and his fragrance and odiferous smell ... it is the honour and ornament
of our English Scepter'. Single roses made of silk and lace were pinned to the bodice or worn
on the shoes. The rose also symbolised the union of York and Lancaster which brought the
Wars of the Roses to an end and established the Tudor dynasty at the end of the 15th century.
Other symbolic flowers include the honeysuckle, the emblem of affection and faithfulness,
while the cherry, the fruit of paradise and reward for virtue, represents heaven. The pansy,
commonly known as heart's-ease, symbol of kind thoughts whose name is derived from the
French *pensée*, made an appropriate motif for use on caps. In *A Midsummer Night's Dream*

29. PORTRAIT OF QUEEN ELIZABETH BY AN UNKNOWN ARTIST *c.* 1590

The blackwork embroidery on the sleeves includes pinks, acorns, roses, honeysuckle, strawberries and borage. The rich effect is enhanced by jewels, one of which can clearly be seen pinned to her left sleeve.

Pollok House, Glasgow.

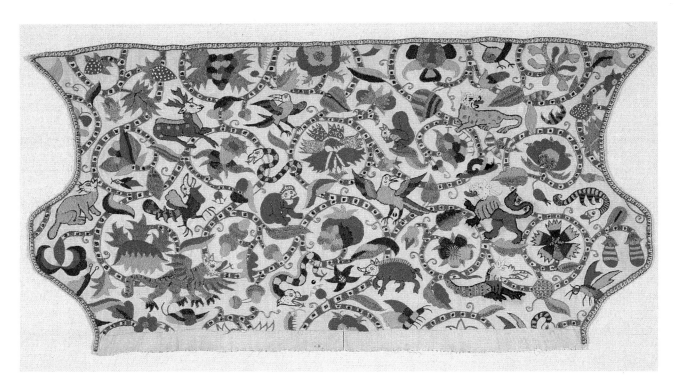

30. COIF, EARLY 17TH CENTURY

Linen worked with silk threads. The colours are unusually vivid and in places two different coloured threads have been twisted together to give an intermediate shade. Various animals, including snakes, are included among the flowers. 23 cm × 45 cm (29/22).

31. (FACING) COIF WITH FOREHEAD CLOTH, EARLY 17TH CENTURY

Embroidered with flowers and fruits, including strawberries and borage which were often depicted together as it was known that they grow better in company with each other. (29/134).

Shakespeare called it Cupid's flower and in *Hamlet* Ophelia says to Laertes: 'There is rosemary, that's for remembrance – pray you, love, remember – and there is pansies that's for thoughts.'

Scrolling patterns in the form of coiling stems are probably a survival of the medieval tradition which often includes birds and animals among the stems. However the 16th- and 17th-century patterns are less sophisticated than the earlier designs as the animals do not form such a well integrated part of the overall design; instead they usually enclose single flowerheads arranged in rows of diagonals. Despite this they have a vital naïve charm emphasised by a lively use of colour.

Among the twenty-six items of embroidered costume in the Collection is a good exam-

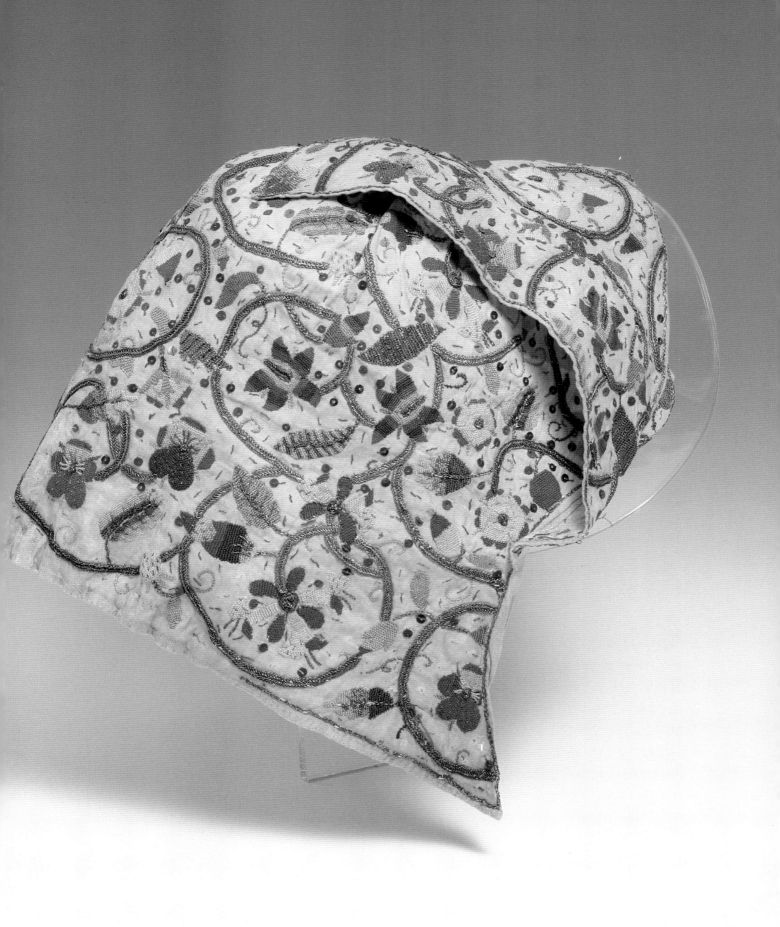

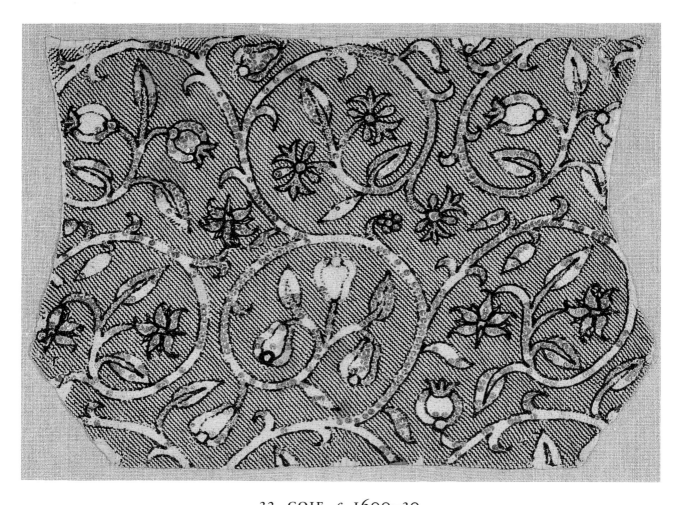

32. COIF, *c.* 1600–30
Worked in black silk threads and spangles, many of which are missing. The small size suggests this may have been worn by a girl. 22.5 cm × 31 cm (29/137).

ple of this type [pl. 30]. It is a woman's cap, known as a coif, which would originally have had a drawstring along the undecorated edge which fitted the back of the neck. Various animals appear among the flowers, some of which are the animal representations of the senses. For example, the dog represents smell, the stag, hearing, the boar, lust and the rather strange human-like monkey eating an apple is taste. There are also heraldic beasts such as the lion and leopard and at the lower right, a wyvern, traditional symbol of cruelty. Coiling among the stems are snakes, which denote wise actions and logic and because of their association with Asclepius, the Greek god of medicine; they also stand for healing. The pomegranate bursting open with an abundance of seeds probably represents fertility. These symbols would originally have been readily understood by the educated, but by the end of the century they had lost much of their significance and become formalised motifs.

Coifs were sometimes worn with a piece of triangular fabric stitched to the front with the point towards the back. These were called forehead cloths and although their exact purpose is uncertain it is known they were worn during illness. Fynnes Morrison wrote in 1617 that 'Many weare such crosse-clothes or forehead clothes as our women use when they are sick'.[9] However, there are only a few examples in paintings of women wearing these caps. The tragic scene of *Sir Thomas Aston at his Wife's Deathbed*, painted in 1635 by John Souch (Manchester Art Galleries), shows Lady Aston, who died in childbirth, wearing a linen cap with a broad lace band covering her forehead. The more cheerful and charming painting of Sir Richard Saltonstall by the bedside of his wife who had recently given birth shows her with a linen cloth covering her forehead. This painting is attributed to David des Granges and is dated about 1638 (Tate Gallery, London).

Although there is no matching forehead cloth with the coif in plate 30, the presence of the symbolic snakes suggests that there may have been one originally. Embroidered coifs and forehead cloths were among the New Year gifts given to Queen Elizabeth by her subjects.

Another coif in the Collection which still has its forehead cloth attached dates from the early years of the 17th century [pl. 31]. It is worked with roses, pansies, strawberries, borage and honeysuckle. The coif and forehead cloth were made separately and then stitched together. Coifs were usually worked in multicoloured silks and although single or bicolours are more unusual there are three examples of this type in the Collection. These may date from the late 16th century. One has simple diagonal bands of blackwork between plain bands decorated with spangles (29/131). Blackwork was monochrome embroidery worked with black silk on white linen in double running, stem, closed herringbone and various filling stitches. It was sometimes enlivened with metal threads or spangles. An interesting blackwork effect was created on another coif [pl. 32] where the scrolling pattern has been defined by the areas left unworked. This is known as voiding. The background has been embroidered densely with diagonal rows of stitches and the unworked areas have been filled with spangles. Blackwork is of Arabic origin and although widely used in the 16th century it had declined in popularity by about 1630. The third coif [pl. 36] is of cream silk, silver and silver-gilt threads worked in scrolling flower motifs.

Men's caps were no less decorative. They were often worked in blackwork enriched with silver and silver-gilt threads or in vividly coloured silks, edged with silver lace and spangles. Spangles were stamped from thin sheets of shiny metal in a variety of shapes and were used to add brilliance to embroidery. They were secured by either a glass bead stitched through a

33. FRAGMENT OF A MAN'S CAP, LATE 16TH OR EARLY 17TH CENTURY

Similar designs are found in Thomas Trevelyon's pattern books. As is often the case, much of the black silk thread has perished because the dye, which is derived from logwood, attacks and weakens it. (29/136).

34. (FACING) MAN'S CAP, EARLY 17TH CENTURY

Linen embroidered with silk and silver threads, with silver spangles and bobbin lace. The flowers and fruit include the daffodil (known as the Lent lily), roses, pansies, honeysuckle, grapes, strawberries and acorns. (29/135).

35. WOMAN'S WAISTCOAT, *c.* 1700
Linen quilted with white silk thread in back stitch and embroidered with silk thread in chain stitch.
Lined with linen. (29/129).

hole or by a knot stitch. The caps were worn indoors as informal wear and were misleadingly known as bedchamber or night caps. (The simple cap worn in bed was called a biggin.) A famous portrait in the National Portrait Gallery, London, of Phineas Pett, the naval architect, painted *c.* 1612, shows him wearing a cap similar to one in the Collection [pl. 34]. Some caps were quilted and may have had lavender or rosemary stitched inside as these were recommended by Gerard 'to comfort the brain' and help recovery from head colds. The floral motifs are the same as those found on women's caps.

The designs for these embroideries must have been readily available as woodcuts and popular prints, but few have survived probably because they simply wore out as a result of frequent use. The outline of a design was transferred to fabric by perforating the paper along the lines of the design with a needle and then by rubbing powdered charcoal or cuttlefish bone, known as pounce, through the holes on to the fabric beneath. The pounce outline was

36. DETAIL OF COIF, *c.* 1600–40
Linen with cut-work, silk threads, and silver and silver-gilt threads in chain stitch in a delicate design
of flowers and birds, edged with silver lace. 21.5 cm × 43 cm (29/130).

55

37. DESIGN SOURCE
Page from *A Booke of Beast, Birds, Flowers, Fruits, Flies and Wormes, exactly drawn with
their Lively Colours truly Described,* a miscellany published by Thomas Johnson in 1630. Grisell Baillie's governess,
May Menzies, traced designs from this book. Property of the Earl of Haddington.

then painted over so that the powder could be safely shaken or blown off. Many of the
designs in pattern books have been perforated in this way.

A collection of patterns which could have been adapted for use on embroidery, plaster-
work or woodcarving was discovered in two commonplace books made by Thomas Trevelyon, a writing master, in the early 1600s.[10] These were for his own use and included
scriveners' alphabets, as well as transcripts from herbals and Topsell's *Book of Beasts*. The
designs are drawn in solid outline with some colour washes and have been copied or traced
from some other source, but many of the designs bear no relationship to embroidery or lace
pattern books of the same date. Included are some designs, similar to those on a fragment of

a man's cap [pl. 34], which could only be for men's caps. They show one segment of the cap which was made from a large single piece of fabric. Either four or six of these shaped sections would be stitched together to form the crown. Some designs also show a suitable border pattern. Others include snakes or serpents similar to those on the coif [pl. 30]. Another design among those intended for embroidery is a shop sign, The Rose and Crown, which is similar to designs found on book covers and also on one of the Burrell samplers (31/1).

By the middle of the 1620s the style of dress began to change. Fashion was led by the court and Charles I's queen Henrietta Maria brought with her the French preference for plainer silks and satins. The taste for embroidered garments declined but gloves and small items such as caps were still worked.

Throughout the century costume continued to be a status symbol and Pepys's diaries are full of references to his purchases of clothes suitable to his and his wife's position. Although embroidered items had gone out of fashion earlier, at the end of the century there was a new interest in quilting which was used for caps and informal waistcoats worn at home by women. These were worked in fine chain stitch in coloured silks on linen and there is a fine example in excellent condition in the Collection [pl. 35].

Some treasured items were occasionally preserved and re-used. Recently during conservation work an embroidered panel on a cushion was found to be a complete late 16th-century coif edged with silver-gilt spangled bobbin lace (29/294a). Rather than cut it up the needlewoman had carefully folded it into a rectangle, stitched it on to red velvet and covered the turned edges with braid.

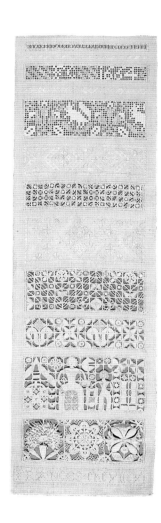

38. (RIGHT) WHITEWORK SAMPLER, 1664
Linen with linen thread in cut and drawn work with needlepoint fillings, detached buttonhole stitches,
raised and padded work. Initialled and dated 'F C 1664' in the second row and 'Frances Cheyney' at the bottom.
65 cm × 20.5 cm (31/22).

39. (LEFT) DETAIL OF SAMPLER [PL.38]
Pink silk has been used for the mouths of the woman and child and the cat between them. (31/22).

CHAPTER 3

THE TRAINING NECESSARY to achieve the high standard of 17th-century embroidery was begun at an early age and needlework formed an increasingly important part of a girl's education. Ralph Verney wrote that his eight-year-old daughter 'being a girl she shall not learn Latin, so she will have more time to learn breeding hereafter and needlework too'.[11] The detailed household accounts kept by Lady Grisell Baillie of Mellerstain House in Scotland record the education of her two daughters in 1707. The instructions for Grisie aged fourteen include:

> To rise by seven a clock and goe about her duty of reading etc etc and be drest and come to breakfast at nine, to play of the spinet till eleven, from eleven till twelve to write and read French, at two a clock to sew her seam till four, at four learn arithmetic, after that dance and play herself until supper and be in bed at nine.[12]

By fourteen Grisie would have been an accomplished needlewoman as she had probably started sewing at the age of six or seven. Girls were sometimes taught embroidery at school but, like many daughters of the aristocracy and gentry, Grisie was taught at home and her governess traced designs for her to work [pl. 37]. From the three surviving dated pieces worked between the ages of eight and thirteen by Martha Edlin (now in the Victoria and Albert Museum, London) we know that a child's first exercise was a band sampler in simple stitches. The format of these narrow samplers with horizontal bands of patterns for borders, alphabets and numbers was established by 1630. They were normally about 20 inches (52 cm) long and between 8 and 12 inches (20.5 cm and 31.5 cm) wide. The edges of the fabric were finished with a narrow border in a different weave known as the selvage. Many of these samplers have the selvage across the top and bottom which shows that they were cut across the width of the linen for reasons of economy. Therefore the maximum length of the sampler was dictated by the width of the loom. These samplers were not for display, but were evidence of the girl's progress and could be kept rolled up in a workbox as a record of patterns and techniques. Before the middle of the century these samplers sometimes include initials and occasionally a name, but only rarely a date.

Samplers must have been made long before the 17th century, but very few that are earlier than 1600 survive. The first printed book of needlework patterns was published in Augsburg in 1523 and there are literary references to samplers in the 16th century. At a time when books were rare samplers must have been an invaluable source of reference for patterns and stitches and were considered important enough by embroiderers to be mentioned in wills.

The border patterns practised on samplers were used to decorate household and personal linen. As wealth increased and households accumulated more goods the linen was embroidered with initials and numbers to enable the lady of the house to keep a check on her supplies. Of the ten band samplers collected by Burrell the earliest date from the 1630s, but most are from the second half of the century. The patterns are of alternating broad and narrow bands of flower and leaf motifs, many identifiable as the thistles, carnations and acorns that had been in use since the 16th century. There are also ancient patterns based on S and X forms. Worked in simple stitches such as cross, stem, double running and eyelet, the embroidery is usually meticulous and the arrangement of closely worked rows gives an effect of richness. Six of these samplers are dated between 1663 and 1686 and each has an additional larger-scale motif worked in the centre. These include huntsmen, a pelican in her piety and a large bunch of stylised flowers. One completed by Jane Turner in 1668 is almost identical to that dated 1667 made by Mary Lawley and now in a Scottish private collection. They both have the same arrangement of patterns and a figure of a woman wearing garments worked in detached buttonhole stitch, just like those made for caskets or pictures. It is possible that both workers attended the same school. However, none of Burrell's dated 17th-century samplers have moralising verses which were introduced at this time and which, together with the over-elaborate border patterns, indicate the changing role of samplers from practical use to schoolroom exercise.

From a band sampler the girl progressed to a more complex and technically demanding cut-work sampler made with white linen threads on white linen [pl. 38]. The first row was fairly straightforward with only a few threads drawn from the fabric on which an open lacy pattern could be created. Then each horizontal band was of increasing complexity until the final row which had squares cut out leaving only a few threads forming a grid. Paper or vellum was often stitched to the back of the fabric to support this grid while the final row was being worked but this was removed when the design was complete. The edges of the cut fabric were finished with overcast stitches and diagonal threads were added to form part of the framework. The delicate, complicated patterns were then built up on the framework using various buttonhole stitches in much the same way as needlepoint lace was made. Three-dimensional effects could be created by working individual pieces such as flower petals separately and then securing them to the sampler with only a few stitches.

Some of the earliest embroidery pattern books contain designs for cut-work. Among the most popular was an English translation of Federigo de Vinciolo's *New and singular patternes and workes of linnen* published in the late 16th century. This exerted great influence and many later books copied it or developed from it. Johann Sibmacher's patterns, originally published in Nuremberg in 1601, were also copied widely. In England between the 1620s and the end of the century more than 150 books of needlework patterns were published.[13] One of the earliest was Richard Shorleyker's *A Schole-house for the Needle* published in 1624. On the title page he claimed: 'Here followeth certaine patterns of cut-workes newly invented and never published before'. This book was very successful, running to twelve editions by 1640. Obviously there was sufficient demand for pattern books to make novelty an important consideration in attracting customers.

Of the twenty-six samplers collected by Burrell, seven are of cut-work and have between eight and twenty-three rows of pattern. One, by Frances Cheyney, consists of eight rows which include squirrels and the figure of a woman and child with a cat [pls 38, 39]. This was completed in 1664, the year after she finished her first band sampler which is also in the Collection (31/20) but unfortunately we do not know what age she was. Very long and elaborate samplers could take up to two years to complete. Two of those in the Burrell Collection are a combination of band patterns and cut and drawnwork. These techniques and patterns were used to decorate bed linen, handkerchiefs, cravats and baby linen.

There was another type of sampler usually associated with the first half of the 17th century, but which was in fact made throughout the period, on which individual motifs or spots were arranged haphazardly. These are unsigned and were probably the practice pieces of experienced embroiderers trying out new techniques, trial designs made before working on a final piece, or just records of designs. Similar motifs can be found on samplers and on finished items. Some of the motifs may originally have been intended for applied work, as it was easier to work individual motifs on separate pieces of fabric and then to cut them out and apply them rather than to work directly on to the finished piece where any mistakes would show. Shorleyker also included 'sundry sorts of spots, as Flowers, Birdes and Fishes etc and will fitly serve to be wrought, some with Gould, some with Silke, and some with Crewell in coullers: or otherwise at your pleasure'. Geometric patterns were also often combined with other motifs.

40. SAMPLER, SECOND HALF OF 17TH CENTURY
Linen with silk and metal threads in a variety of rococo, chain, satin and eyelet stitches with French knots. Said to
have been worked by Mary of Modena. 43 cm × 58.5 cm (31/10).

A good example of the combination of geometric motifs with flowers and birds was
bought by Burrell in 1925 [pl. 40]; formerly in the collection of the Countess of Ranfurly, it
is said to be by Maria d'Este (1658–1718), known as Mary of Modena, second wife of James,
Duke of York, later James VII and II (1633–1701). The geometric patterns are similar to those
on a needlework chair cover in the Fitzwilliam Museum, Cambridge, which is also said to be
the work of Maria d'Este.

The culmination of a girl's needlework education involved working several small
pictorial panels drawn out on one piece of fabric which, when complete, would be sent to a
cabinetmaker to be made up into a box or casket [pls 41, 42]. Each picture for the sides, top

and drawer fronts would be mounted separately on to the wood and the edges hidden with silver gimp or braid. Finally silver lock-plates and handles, and silvered wooden feet would be fitted. That so many survive no doubt has as much to do with their being treasured for sentimental reasons, or because they were silver, as for their decorative quality. One casket in the Collection [pl. 79] is unusual in being worked on paper rather than the more usual satin.

Simple small rectangular boxes covered in canvas work, of which there are three in the Collection, were made earlier in the 17th century but larger, more elaborate caskets were popular during the second half of the century. They were of two types: rectangular boxes with flat lids, and those known as double caskets or cabinets which usually had double doors at the front opening to reveal a series of small shallow drawers. The top was hinged and had sloping sides. Inside were divisions for perfume bottles or an inkwell, sandbox and pen-tray. Occasionally a mirror was fitted under the lid and on the very rare occasion a three-dimensional garden with ivory figures. Sometimes the drawers are lined with printed or painted

41. SIDE OF A CASKET, DATED 1659

Paris offers the golden ball to Venus. Satin worked with silks in long and short, stem, chain and split stitches with couching, laid and tied fillings. The inside of the casket is lined with pink silk and fitted with trays. On the underside of the lid is a space for a mirror. See also plate 61.   26 cm × 30 cm (29/229).

42. BACK OF A CASKET, *c.* 1650–80

The man holds a Bible, the child a bird of carved wood and the woman a flower. Raised and padded work with
silk and metal threads, metal purls, beads and lace. Two other almost identical versions are known: one in laid silks
is in the Lady Lever Gallery, Liverpool; the other in tent stitch, dated 1657, is illustrated in Huish's
Samplers and Tapestry Embroideries, London 1900.   13.5 cm × 25 cm (29/169).

paper, but more often with plain pink silk. These cabinets are similar in construction and
many have the same secret drawer. The earliest dated example is in the Whitworth Gallery,
Manchester, and it contains a letter written by Hannah Smith in 1657 recording the making
of her cabinet which she completed when she was almost twelve.

The subjects chosen to decorate these cabinets and many other objects were often biblical as the Bible was central to 17th-century life and in particular to the Protestant ethic. Although the first readily available English translation of the Bible was authorised by James VI and I and published in 1611, many illustrated Bibles were imported earlier from northern Europe following the Reformation. These provided the sources for many embroidery designs such as one casket in the Collection depicting scenes from the life of Isaac (29/166). However, on occasions scenes from different stories are combined. Many of the stories included heroines such as Judith, Abigail, Esther and Susanna who saved others by their courageous actions. These heroines were celebrated for their virtue and depicted throughout the 16th and 17th centuries in a variety of media ranging from painting and enamels to ceramics. They were also the inspiration for books such as Thomas Heywood's *The Exemplary Lives and Memorable Acts of Nine of the Most Worthy Women of the World*. They were considered suitable embroidery subjects and may have been admired by the embroiderers who perhaps perceived links between the actions of these heroines and the activity of women during the Civil War and Commonwealth. Although there had been some minor changes in the role and status of women as a result of the economic issues involved in marriage as the middle classes sought to establish their position through the acquisition of land and property, most women continued to be confined to domestic occupations. However the Civil War did force many women to assume responsiblities for their families' estates and businesses. They travelled more widely, particularly during a husband's exile or imprisonment, when they petitioned Parliament for the return of sequestered property. Yet despite the necessity of their involvement in business, which was not recognised in law, this activity gave rise to anxiety, especially among Puritans who saw it as a threat to the stability of family life. The importance placed on fidelity and the family by the Puritans is reflected in the biblical subject matter of embroideries.

Although it is rare to find panels depicting only mythological stories some have survived that combine mythological and biblical subjects. One flat-topped casket in Burrell's Collection, dated 1659, has on the top the sacrifice of Isaac and on the front a huntsman and hounds in pursuit of a stag, oblivious of Daedalus watching as his son Icarus, with melting wings, plunges to earth above them. The moral conveyed by Icarus's fate is that we must be wary not to overreach ourselves. Another side of the casket portrays Paris choosing between Juno, Venus and Minerva, watched by Cupid from the edge of the lid [pl. 41].

Many of these caskets are in raised work which is better known as stump work, a term that only came into use in the 19th century. This exuberant form of embroidery was worked in other countries and at earlier times, but is particularly associated with English secular

43. MAN AND WOMAN IN A GARDEN, SECOND HALF OF 17TH CENTURY
Raised and padded work on satin ground. The raised work fruit has first been worked in long and short stitch to
enhance the three-dimensional effect. Around the man and woman are various symbols. Beside the woman
are a peacock for pride and a harpy for avarice, and beside the man is a cockatrice for lust. Avarice and lust
were considered the two most deadly sins. Between the couple is the fountain of spirituality and harmony
represented by music. 34 cm × 48 cm (29/99).

embroidery of the third quarter of the 17th century when it was used in a distinctly lively
manner by young girls.

The images would be made individually and then applied to the satin ground which
usually has three green stripes in the selvage. The raised areas were padded with wool or
hemp, or whatever came to hand. Figures often had detached lace-stitched garments with
seed pearls, coral beads or lace trimmings [pls 42, 81]. Occasionally feathers were added as
another contrasting texture. The head and hands were usually of wood, either painted or
covered with satin, although the hands could also be made of wire wrapped with thread.

Sometimes the designs on the satin were worked first in flat stitches and the individual raised motifs stitched on top to give an even greater three-dimensional appearance.

Laid work was used to decorate the drawers, but was also applied to the exterior panels. Its use called for great flair in the control of colour to create the effect of shading which gives a distinctive yet subtle appearance. There are four of these cabinets in the Collection, two with sloping tops.

Several different techniques were often combined in a single piece, as described by John Taylor in *The Needle's Excellency*.

44. MIRROR CASE, *c.* 1650–80
Satin with multicoloured beads, silk and metal threads
and metal purl in raised and padded work.
39 cm × 43.5 cm (29/115).

For Tent-worke, Raised-work, Laid-work, Frost-work, Net-worke,
Most Curious Purles, or rare Italian Cut-worke,
Fine Ferne-stitch, Fisher-stitch, Irish-stitch, and Queen-stitch,
The Spanish-stitch, Rosemary-stitch, and Mowse-stitch,
The smarting Whip-stitch, Back-stitch, and the Crosse-stitch,
All these are good, and these we must allow,
And these are everywhere in practise now.

Two of Burrell's caskets which at first glance look very different from each other have virtually identical arrangements of the same designs. The difference is that one is worked in flat stitches and more subdued colours than the other which is in vividly coloured raised work. Although the designs for these caskets were sold as standard sets their interpretation into embroidery presented a creative challenge to the embroiderer. Individuality of execution was achieved by the choice of stitches and colours, and it is possible on several pieces, where the drawing is exposed, to see how much the final result differs from the form originally outlined.

Pictures worked on white satin became popular at the same time as the caskets. These pictures were similar to those intended for caskets, only larger, and they depict the same biblical subjects based on the same designs. However, a distinctive type now emerges of a man and a woman standing in a pleasure garden and although there are minor variations between pictures the basic elements remain fairly constant [pl. 43]. The man often carries his hat and the woman is usually carrying a book or Bible, or is offering him a flower. In the Collection there are two examples of this type and in both the figures stand on either side of an elaborate fountain and grotto. Fountains were fashionable elements of garden architecture at the time. Heraldic animals sometimes appear among the flora and fauna surrounding the figures, and they may have emblematic meaning. On the other hand they may simply have been inspired by the carved beasts set on painted posts which were decorative features in some gardens in the 16th and first half of the 17th century. Occasionally an arbour is included supporting sweet-smelling plants. Such arbours provided a sheltered place to sit and a welcome change from the rather foul-smelling indoors. These pictures on white satin may celebrate an engagement or marriage, with the couple shown in an Arcadian garden of love, but here secular and religious meanings overlap. The garden of love is linked to ideas of Paradise and the peacock is both the symbol of pride and of the Resurrection. Such layers of meaning in poetry and pictures would have been readily understood by the educated of the time.

Instead of applying their raised work to caskets, girls might have chosen to use it to embellish frames for mirrors that began to appear in better-off households. An inventory

45. MIRROR, 1670S

Embroidered border within a tortoiseshell mount. The raised and padded figures represent Charles II and Queen
Catherine of Braganza. There are traces of feathers on their robes which were used to represent ermine.
The figures in the corners representing the seasons include for winter the same design used on a box in the
Collection [pl. 49]. The mirror was formerly in the collection of Percival Griffiths of
Castle Hedingham, Essex. 105.5 cm × 81 cm (29/224).

46. BEADWORK BASKET, *c.* 1675

Said to have been made by Elizabeth Clarke (1655–99) when she was about twenty years old. These baskets may
have been made to celebrate betrothals and used to hold gloves or sprigs of rosemary given to wedding guests.
50 cm × 63 cm (29/176).

made at Hardwick Hall as early as 1601 mentions a looking glass with a border of embroidery.
The mirrors were usually hung above, or stood on, a dressing table with a sconce or candlestick at each side to provide light. Some mirrors were fitted with feet similar to those on the
caskets and these lay flat on the dressing table. To protect them, the mirrors had padded
hinged covers which were usually embroidered [pl. 44].

All three frames collected by Burrell have a figure on each side of the mirror with an
elaborate building or portrait at the top, and either flowers, animals or representations of the

seasons in the four corners. This is the most commonly found composition on embroidered frames and may be derived from the decoration on the title pages of books with the mirror in place of the lettering.[14] The frames were occasionally of elaborate scallop shapes or were contained within an outer frame of tortoiseshell.

On two of the frames in the Collection the figures are in raised work and may represent Charles II and his queen Catherine of Braganza [pl. 45]. Royal personages and biblical figures such as King Solomon and the Queen of Sheba are often depicted beneath tented canopies or baldachins in 17th-century needlework. The striking resemblance between the embroidered kings and portraits of Charles II suggests that the embroidered images were derived from contemporary prints of Charles and Catherine. Prior to recent research on the sources of embroidery designs, it was said that most figures of kings and queens were either Charles I and Henrietta Maria or Charles II and Catherine of Braganza. This identification may have been correct, or it may have been a spurious means of inflating the price of an embroidery.

Popular prints supplied a wide variety of motifs. The old man by the fire, who was frequently used in medieval calendars, manuscripts and stained glass to personify winter, also appears in several 17th-century embroideries. This figure may have been derived from a series of popular prints representing the seasons by Wenceslas Hollar, which was first published in 1640 and copied by others. The same figure appears on the beadwork box [pl. 49] which has another panel with a female figure with a sheaf of corn and a scythe who represents Ceres or summer. The figure of Flora represents spring, and the figure of Bacchus autumn. The figures of winter and summer also appear on the sides of Hannah Smith's casket in the Whitworth Art Gallery, Manchester.

Beadwork was another form of needlework associated with the second half of the 17th century. It was often used on mirror frames and was combined with other techniques in the working of the same designs as those used for silk threads. Burrell collected seven items made completely from glass beads. There are two panels, one of King Solomon receiving the Queen of Sheba and the other with motifs of birds, animals, flowers, a shepherd and shepherdess. On these the beads have been stitched to a silk satin ground in a straightforward method of execution. Although beads do not fade, extant pieces of beadwork are often in poor condition because the weight and hardness of the glass have abraded the supporting fabric and threads.

More complex in construction were the embroidered baskets of which there are two in the Collection. One has a female figure contained within an oval framework with birds, vases of flowers and heraldic animals around the sides. More striking is the large rectangular

47. (LEFT) PAIR OF BELLOWS, DATED 1673
Worked in beads on satin with the figure worked in silk thread. The reverse has a vase of flowers and the date.
Red beads were the most expensive and were used sparingly. 57 cm × 26 cm (29/223).

48. (RIGHT) GLASS PANEL, ENGLISH, LATE 15TH CENTURY
Labour of the month roundel showing February, probably from a set formerly in the old parsonage of
St Michael-at-Coslany in Norwich. Three others are in the Victoria and Albert Museum, London.
Diameter 23.5 cm (45/429).

basket, the satin base of which is decorated with the image of a woman offering a flower to a man [pl. 46]. These figures are contained within an arbour. The sides of the basket are decorated with three-dimensional flowers and fruit and the decorative trefoil handles are also covered in beads. In the most finely worked areas each bead is threaded individually and looped to the bead in the row above to create solid shapes. These were then wired to support the free-standing motif.

As many baskets exist, and as they are often similar to the silver layette baskets used for baby clothes, it has been suggested that they may have been made to commemorate christenings.[15] However, as many depict a man and a woman, it seems more likely that these were made for use at wedding ceremonies to hold gloves which were given as gifts or favours to special guests – in much the same way as flowers or good luck charms from wedding cakes (which we still call favours) are given today.

In Italy glass beads had been threaded and used in relief since the 14th century and in the exotic fantasy tale *Hypnerotomachia Poliphili*, published in 1499, there are references to flowers made of tiny pearls or beads with silk leaves. Tiny roses are described as being so perfectly executed that they are more real than reality. As the technique of making glass beads spread to France so the technique of using them in embroidery spread to convents and private houses throughout northern Europe.[16]

Unlike silks, the glass beads do not fade. The choice of colour was restricted, with blue,

49. SIDE OF A BOX, LATE 17TH CENTURY

Worked completely in beads apart from the old man's hat which may have been of more perishable material such as feathers, or the beads were secured with black thread which has decayed. Derived from a traditional medieval figure, the old man sits incongruously before his fire in a leafy landscape. 20 cm × 42 cm (29/234).

yellow and green being most widely used. Red is found less frequently as it was the most expensive. A number of household articles were decorated with beads. The Collection includes a frame with a padded cover protecting a small mirror decorated with the figures of a king and queen surrounded by flowers which is very similar to pieces in the Lady Lever Gallery, Liverpool, the Royal Museum of Scotland, Edinburgh, and the Metropolitan Museum, New York. More unusual is a pair of bellows decorated in beadwork with the figure of a woman on one side and on the reverse a vase of flowers and the date 1673 [pl. 47]. They were purchased in 1934 and were formerly in the collection of Percival Griffiths.

Another handsome piece is a flat-topped ebony box with beadwork on a linen ground depicting the seasons [pl. 49]. The front represents summer, the back spring and the side depicting winter has the same design as that used on one of the mirrors. The lid has an unidentified coat of arms. Large square boxes, either decorated with beads or of walnut with an embroidered panel on the top, protected by glass, were made in the 1690s. They are thought to have been used to store lace which had become very fashionable for elaborate headdresses.

CHAPTER 4

◆ THEMES IN CANVAS WORK PICTURES ◆

HAVING DEMONSTRATED their proficiency young women would progress to the fine canvas work pictures which were probably made in imitation of large tapestries. It may have been this association with tapestries which particularly appealed to Burrell as he bought thirty-one examples of canvas work, the largest group within the embroidery collection.

Tapestry workshops were set up at Mortlake on the Thames in 1619 and their products were highly valued, but beyond the means of all but the wealthiest for use in the grandest houses. Small canvas work pictures were introduced in the 1630s and provided alternative decorative elements for the flat areas of panelling in rooms where their garish colours would glow against the dark wood. These pictures have their origins in the bed valances of the late 16th century which were decorated with biblical and mythological scenes, gardens and rural landscapes full of birds and animals. Both professionals and amateurs made sets of valances using green, blue, yellow and red wools on coarse linen canvas. These sets were major undertakings and although the decorative pictures are on a much smaller scale the concentration needed to complete those worked on the finest linen was considerable. Some demanded as many as 1,600 stitches per square inch compared with 400 on the coarser canvas of furnishings [pls 50, 51, 52]. The variety of stitches used is limited when compared to the elaborate embroidery on garments made early in the 17th century, but there is a vivacity about the pictures which belies the apparently painstaking and repetitive work. The vivid colours, still seen on the unfaded reverse of the embroideries, must have contributed considerably to their lively appearance.

Canvas work was a popular form of needlework throughout the 17th century and the subjects depicted include stories and fanciful images that were familiar to the young worker and would appeal to her imagination. For example, it is not surprising that the grotto with a mermaid combing her hair before a mirror was a popular subject, as it appeared frequently

50. PANEL DEPICTING DAVID AND ABIGAIL, 1640–60

The central rose with two distinctly different leaves is a reference to the conflict between the Parliamentarians and the Royalists. An unfinished panel of similar design, in the Untermyer Collection in the Metropolitan Museum of Art, New York, has a dominant oak tree in place of the rose as an obvious mark of allegiance. On both panels the horses at the top right have two heads, but only two front legs between them and no hind quarters, suggesting that the original pattern was carelessly drawn. 31 cm × 40 cm (29/71).

51. (FACING) DETAIL OF DAVID AND ABIGAIL [PL. 50] 1640–60

Linen worked in tent, long and short stitches with couched threads. The windows are of mica. The work is incredibly fine with over 2,000 stitches per square inch. Detail 19 cm × 15.5 cm (29/71).

52. REVERSE OF DAVID AND ABIGAIL [PL.50]
The brilliance of the original colours is very evident on this side of the panel. (29/71).

in children's books such as Overton's *A New Book of all Sorts of Beasts: or a pleasant Way to teach Yeoung Children to Reade almost as soon as Speake*, published in 1671. Randle Holme's *Academy of Armoury*, published in 1688, included similar mermaids and they could also be found decorating large dishes and wood carvings [pls 53, 54]. In the Victoria and Albert Museum, London, there is a silver ewer in the form of a mermaid made in London in 1610; the basin is in the form of a silver scallop shell. Mermaids were regarded as beautiful but dangerous creatures who lured sailors to their death. Beauty was often viewed with suspicion as a sign of sexual voracity and as mermaids are usually shown combing their hair and holding a mirror they may represent Vanitas – a warning to young women [pl. 53]. Other moral messages were conveyed by pictures derived from emblem books and prints.

With the development and improvement in printing techniques books became more accessible during the 16th century. Woodcuts and copper engravings illustrated mythological, classical and biblical stories and became so popular that they continued to be reprinted until the middle of the 17th century. Many Bibles and books were published in France and Germany but the majority originated in Flanders and the Netherlands.

Plates by various artists were collected together in individual volumes. Among the most successful of such books was the two-volume *Thesaurus Sacrarum Historiarum Veteris Testamenti* (Dictionary of Sacred Stories from the Old Testament) published in Antwerp in 1585 by Gerard de Jode [pls 55, 58, 59, 72]. Many of the engravings are after paintings by the Flemish artist Martin de Vos (1531–1603) which inspired 17th-century needlewomen to show their skill. Some of these engravings were later published by Dutch printsellers in the 1650s.

53. (LEFT) DETAIL OF PANEL [PL. 21], MID 17TH CENTURY
Tiny mermaids complete with comb and mirror are often depicted in needlework pictures. Occasionally the mirrors are of mica, but here the reflection is embroidered (29/49).

54. (RIGHT) DETAIL OF PANELLING, HUTTON CASTLE DINING ROOM, *c.* 1500
This panelling is thought to have come originally from Harrington Hall, Lincolnshire. The motifs used in embroidery were also widely used in other media.

Cum puero Ismaële procul, dimittitur Hagar, Quem Sara hæredem noluit eße suum.   Genes. 21.

55. ABRAHAM BANISHES HAGAR AND ISHMAEL

Engraving from Gerard de Jode, *Thesaurus Sacrarum Historiarum Veteris Testamenti*, Antwerp 1585.

Courtesy of the Trustees of the National Library of Scotland.

56. PANEL DEPICTING THE STORY OF HAGAR AND ISHMAEL, 1630–60

Sarah and Isaac watch as Abraham banishes his son Ishmael with the Egyptian servant Hagar, his mother, into the desert. Hagar carries food and water. In the background Ishmael lies dying, but an angel shows Hagar a well nearby. This is one of two panels in the Collection depicting such scenes which are common in 17th-century Dutch and Italian art. The relationship between men and women was a topic of much debate at the time.

29 cm × 42.5 cm (29/48).

Parituram Saram nunciant Abrahæ angeli hospites: Saræque ridenti, promissionis verba reterant. Genes. 18.

57. ABRAHAM OFFERS HOSPITALITY TO THE ANGELS
Engraving from Gerard de Jode, *Thesaurus Sacrarum Historiarum Veteris Testamenti,* Antwerp 1585.
Courtesy of the Trustees of the National Library of Scotland

58. PANEL DEPICTING ABRAHAM OFFERING HOSPITALITY TO THE ANGELS, 1630–60
Worked in wool on linen canvas. The angels tell of the birth of a son to his elderly wife, Sarah. The angels represent
the Trinity and the scene prefigures the Annunciation. 40.5 cm × 48 cm (29/43).

Potum dat Rebecca seruo Abrahæ, eiusque camelis: Vnde cognoscitis preparasse hanc Dominum hero suo coniugem. Genes.

59. REBECCA AND ELIEZER AT THE WELL
Engraving from Gerard de Jode, *Thesaurus Sacrarum Historiarum Veteris Testamenti,* Antwerp 1585.
Courtesy of the Trustees of the National Library of Scotland.

60. PANEL SHOWING REBECCA AT THE WELL *c.* 1650–80

This panel forms the top of a casket. Other scenes from the life of Isaac decorate the sides. Subjects such as this and particularly those relating to the search for a suitable wife were popular for boxes. 14 cm × 20 cm (29/165).

Favourite designs recur in embroidered panels, mainly from the Old Testament and Old Testament Apochrypha. Of Burrell's three panels depicting Abraham casting aside Hagar and Ishmael, two are derived from the *Thesaurus Sacrarum*. There are at least fifteen known panels from this source [pls 56, 58].[17]

The story of Abraham and Isaac was a popular subject and was told in six engravings of which the incident with Hagar is the second. The first shows Abraham kneeling before three angels who tell him that his wife Sarah will have a son. There are three examples of this in the Collection, one on a bed valance (29/44) of the late 16th or early 17th century, one on a cushion (29/191) and the third an embroidered panel [pl. 58] from the middle of the century. However, although the embroidered panel is very similar to de Jode's engraving of the scene there are a number of distinct differences, which would suggest a different source. In the embroidery Sarah stands in a tent rather than in a doorway and the angels are standing whereas two are seated at a table in de Jode's version. The third scene shows the dramatic moment when the sacrifice of Isaac is averted by an angel. Occasionally these three scenes are combined in one panel as in the Untermyer Collection in the Metropolitan Museum, New York, but in the Burrell Collection they remain separate. The sacrifice and the remaining three scenes are illustrated on a casket (29/166) bought in 1934. Scenes four to six show Abraham sending his servant Eliezer, with his camel, to find a wife for Isaac, Eliezer's meeting with Rebecca at the well [pl. 60], and finally the meeting of Isaac and Rebecca [pl. 79]. The themes of marriage and obedience were considered particularly appropriate for an adolescent girl completing her needlework education [pl. 61].

Subjects illustrating dramatic moments from favourite stories and derived from these 16th-century engravings recur in other media. Many of the small Sheldon tapestries were woven with these designs (there are nineteen in the Collection). The bold, vividly coloured tapestries made as book cushions or sets of covers for chair cushions were produced at Barcheston, Warwickshire, where the first commercial tapestry workshop was established in 1561 by William Sheldon, a country gentleman and a successful wool trader.

The canvas work pictures shared many subjects in common with contemporary paintings although it is not always easy to compare the two media. For example, the moment in the story of the sacrifice of Isaac when the angel stops the downsweep of Abraham's sword was a popular subject with painters of the time, including Rembrandt. It can also be seen on Sheldon tapestries and large decorative tin-glazed earthenware dishes. These dishes, some of which were known as blue-dash chargers from the borders of slanting, blue brushstrokes, were displayed on large, handsome oak cupboards and, like the embroideries and Sheldon tapestries, added a colourful, decorative note to the dark furniture. Bold colours would have

61. PANEL SHOWING THE SACRIFICE OF ISAAC, DATED 1659

This panel is from the top of the box illustrated in plate 41. There was a strict hierarchy within the family and this popular subject was a dramatic reminder of the importance of obedience to both the head of the family and to God. 30 cm × 26 cm (29/229).

been an advantage in the dark interiors during winter and at night, as good wax candles were expensive and most light would have come from the fire.

Many subjects can be interpreted in several ways. Illustrations of New Testament stories were thought to smack of popery and so Old Testament stories prefiguring episodes in the life of Christ were often preferred. Needlework pictures based on the life of Christ are rare but there are two in the Collection, one showing the raising of Lazarus [pl. 62], and the other, Mary Magdalene washing Christ's feet (29/79). Some of the subjects may also be allusions to contemporary events. For example the judgement of Solomon possibly prefigures the Last Judgement but the dispute between the two women may represent the struggle between king and state. Another possible interpretation is that it represents the wisdom of the monarchy alluding to the divine right of kings at a time when the issue of monarchy was central to political discussion. It is often said that these pictures are full of Royalist symbols: the caterpillar is the badge of Charles I; the acorn and oak leaves stand for Charles II and the butterfly for his restoration. While this may be true, all of these motifs were widely used in earlier embroideries and we should be wary of reading too much significance into stock figures and traditional motifs. However, as subjects with hidden meanings seem to have been particularly popular during the 1640s and 50s, when several images are used together, the cumulative evidence is convincing.

One such panel from the 1650s shows the figure of Charles I, derived from a popular print, heroically dressed in armour and standing in front of a campaign tent decked with flags [pl. 63]. To one side of him is an oak tree, probably representing the Boscobel oak which sheltered Charles II after the Battle of Worcester. On the other side the woman playing a lute suggests the harmony of the monarchy, while above her flies a butterfly, which in this context may well refer to the wished-for Restoration. The castle may hint at Charles I's imprisonment before his death and the sun above, emerging from behind a cloud, may represent Truth, as everything is revealed by its light. There are so few plants in this embroidery that those included – a thistle, tulip and acorn – were surely chosen judiciously.

The period of the Civil War was a traumatic time for the country, when one man in ten was under arms and members of the same family were often on opposite sides. Although many seditious pamphlets and satirical prints were published embroideries with overt political themes are rare. There are two derived from an anti-Catholic print 'The Double Deliverance'[18] and embroidered portraits of the king were copied from his self-vindication, *The Eikon Basilike – The Portrait of his sacred Majesty in his Solitude and Sufferings*, which was published posthumously. Burrell acquired a copy of this 17th-century bestseller for his Collection. Surprisingly he did not buy a single embroidered portrait (which had been

62. PANEL SHOWING THE RAISING OF LAZARUS, MID 17TH CENTURY
The initials MML on the tomb probably refer to Martha, Mary and Lazarus. Mary Magdalene is shown as an unrepentant, exotically dressed courtesan, possibly representing profane love. Beside her is her plainly dressed sister Martha, patroness of housewives, holding a domestic utensil or keys. The figures behind may represent Mary after her conversion and Martha weeping over her dead brother. 31.5 cm × 48 cm (29/74).

popular with Royalist sympathisers) although one was for sale in the exhibition at which he bought the hawking accoutrements, the bellows, a casket and a mirror.

During such times of political and religious upheaval it is not surprising that the central characters in many of the pictures were women famed for their heroism. A favourite was Queen Esther who, through her influence over her husband, saved her people at great risk to herself. There are four versions in the Collection. One, dated 1652, depicts the whole story of the plot to destroy the Jews by Haman, vizier to the Persian king Ahasuerus [pl. 64]. At the top right the sleepless king has the record of events read to him and is told of the part played by Mordecai (Queen Esther's cousin) in foiling a plot against him. Mordecai is rewarded by being dressed in the king's finest clothes and can be seen on horseback following a herald to the palace. On the left the king and Haman attend a banquet organised by Queen Esther, at which Esther denounces Haman who is subsequently hanged on the gallows he had prepared for Mordecai. In the centre is the dramatic moment when the king touches Esther with his golden sceptre to grant her request for the right of self-defence for her people. Had he refused her request he would have condemned her to death.

This subject was depicted widely in embroidery made during the 1640s and 50s, and may, in its reference to persecuted minorities, hint at the political or religious sympathies of the embroiderer. A feminist interpretation suggests that it alludes to women themselves. A particularly important version in the Collection appears to be a strongly political statement [pl. 65]. We do not know who executed it, but the date 1648, the year of the second civil war, is worked boldly in seed pearls. Above the king are the arms of the Crispe family who were from Bramfield in Suffolk. The counties of Lincolnshire, East Anglia and Suffolk were strongly Puritan from early in the 17th century and had suffered religious intolerance under James VI and I. As a result the Pilgrim Fathers sailed from Boston, Lincolnshire, to seek freedom of worship in America. Later, Suffolk was one of the counties united by Parliament in the Eastern Association which controlled all the resources of farming, trade and industry. This association was of vital importance to the Parliamentary cause and a leading light was Oliver Cromwell, country gentleman and MP for Cambridge. Suffolk suffered particularly badly from Cromwell's iconoclasm and during the 1640s the Royalist minority must have had a difficult time, particularly at the siege of Colchester in 1648, when they were treated very harshly. An account of this 'great and bloudy fight' was published the same year and may have contributed to the subtle declaration of allegiance on the embroidered panel.[19]

The panel is based on an engraving by Martin van Heemskerk (1498–1574) who was the first major Netherlandish artist to design specifically for printmakers. The original design shows the figures in exotic dress, but in this embroidered panel the costume has been adapted. All the figures wear civilian clothes except Esther who is shown in Roman armour of the type designed by Inigo Jones for court masques. Roman wives were renowned for their martial spirit and although this is an obvious allusion to Esther's bravery it is in all probability a hidden reference to the bravery shown by women during the Civil War. For example, the Countess of Portland was likened to a Roman matron during the defence of Carisbrooke Castle and many other noblewomen such as Lady Bankes and Brilliana Lady Harley were celebrated for their heroism in refusing to surrender their castles under siege while their husbands were absent.[20]

There are two other known embroideries derived from this source. The large hanging attributed to Mary Jamesone in St Nicholas Kirk, Aberdeen, is closest to the engraving.[21]

63. PANEL WITH FIGURE OF CHARLES I, 1650S

This embroidery proclaims the heroic nature of the martyr Charles I and calls for the restoration of the harmony of the monarchy. It symbolises the conflict of the time. On the left is harmony and on the right discord, represented by the campaign tents of the battlefield. 27 cm × 33 cm (29/106).

The other, in the Untermyer Collection in the Metropolitan Museum of Art, New York, depicts the scene in a landscape rather than an architectural setting.

According to a survey by Charlotte Mayhew, Esther and Ahasuerus is the most commonly found subject on embroidered pictures.[22] Another panel of this subject embroidered with the arms of the Dyers Company and the date 1654 is in the Ashmolean Museum, Oxford. The year 1654 saw the end of the first Dutch war which was essentially a trade war. The embroidery may refer to this or to events concerning the Dyers Company, which during the austerity of the Commonwealth may well have been suffering hardship. Apprentices had been involved in protests at various times throughout the troubles. In Norwich they protested against the repressive measures of the Puritan city fathers, and in the Skinners Hall, London, apprentices were involved in signing a *Solemn Engagement* pressing for the king's restoration to power.

It is important that these embroideries should be seen in their widest cultural, social and political context and not simply as the chance product of leisured young women. Every embroidered detail should be studied with care to identify anomalies which may contribute to an understanding of the piece. For example, in plate 56 by the side of the pool there is a rose supporting an oak leaf and an acorn – a detail that could easily be overlooked – but in this statement of allegiance the embroiderer demonstrates her awareness of political events.

Among other things, social disruption gave everyone opportunities for heroic action. Mary Overton withstood harassment, public humiliation and imprisonment when she was arrested with her brother, the publisher Thomas Johnson, for stitching the sheets of a seditious pamphlet. In 1649 she petitioned the House of Commons for the release of her husband, the brother of publisher Henry Overton, with the wives of other men imprisoned for their democratic and levelling ideas.[23] Abigail, the biblical heroine who interceded on behalf of her husband in order to save him from David's revenge, must have struck a chord with many women during the 1640s and 50s. She is among the most popular figures embroidered at this time.

Other biblical characters who played an influential role in events and who could be considered as role models were Ruth, Esther, Rebecca, Abigail and the Queen of Sheba. Heroines such as Judith, who beheaded the Assyrian general Holofernes, were to be admired for their prowess and valour rather than emulated. All of these women are frequently portrayed in canvas work pictures. Womanly virtues were encouraged in scenes such as the finding of Moses [pl. 66] and the plight of Hagar and Ishmael [pl. 56] which demonstrate the responsible and influential role of women in marriage. A moral message about the importance of virtue and chastity and warnings about the evils of immorality were inherent

64. PANEL WITH THE STORY OF ESTHER AND AHASUERUS, DATED 1652

The lion depicted is not the usual benevolent heraldic lion, but has a bloody bone in its mouth and in front of its paws are bones gnawed clean. This adds to the political symbolism of the subject. The initials IH are worked on the tablecloth at the left, on the top of the central pavilion. IH and the date appear on the house at the top. Apart from small details this panel is identical to another in the Ashmolean Museum, Oxford, which bears the arms of the Dyers' Company. 42 cm × 51 cm (29/64).

65. PANEL SHOWING ESTHER AND AHASUERUS, DATED 1648

Political sympathies are expressed in this panel in which the virtuous Esther, who probably represents a vulnerable minority, overcomes evil. This is the most common subject found on canvas work pictures. The date 1648 is worked prominently in seed pearls. This was the year of the second Civil War and according to the old calendar then in use it was also the year Charles I was beheaded. The king was executed on 30 January but before 1752 (when the Gregorian calendar was adopted in Britain) each year began in March. 30.5 cm × 37.5 cm (29/72).

in the stories of Susannah and the elders and of David and Bathsheba. There are three fine panels in the Collection depicting Bathsheba whose story was also told in 17th-century broadside ballads.

In the 16th and 17th centuries Susannah was the most popular biblical heroine, partly because she personified virtue, and partly because she provided an opportunity to depict a naked, voluptuous female [pls 67–69]. Tintoretto, Veronese, Rubens, Jordaens, Rembrandt and many other major artists painted versions of the story. Susannah, the wife of a prosperous Jew, was desired by two elders who tried to seduce her while she bathed. Despite their threats to denounce her as an adulteress (for which the penalty was death) unless she complied, she refused and called for help. When the elders carried out their threat Daniel proved

66. PANEL DEPICTING MOSES DISCOVERED BY PHARAOH'S DAUGHTER, *c.* 1650–80
Satin ground with raised work. The figures in the foreground have wooden faces and hands, and the woman in the background is unpadded. There are two portraits in the upper corners, a woman on the left and a man on the right. The grotto is heavily encrusted with coral, shells, beads and crystal. 30.5 cm × 43 cm (29/56).

67. PANEL DEPICTING SUSANNAH AND THE ELDERS, *c.* 1630–60

The story is told in five scenes based on four engravings from Gerard de Jode's *Thesaurus Sacrarum Historiarum
Veteris Testamenti*, Antwerp 1585. It is unusual for the whole story to be depicted. There is an identical panel in the
Untermyer Collection, Metropolitan Museum of Art, New York. 36 cm × 44.5 cm (29/62).

68. CUSHION COVER WITH SUSANNAH AND THE ELDERS, SHORTLY AFTER 1603
This cushion cover is attributed to the Sheldon workshop. 48.5 cm × 51 cm (47/10).

69. CHARGER DEPICTING SUSANNAH AND THE ELDERS, DATED 1648
An example of this subject used in another medium. The rim is decorated with mermaids which are often found in
children's books and embroideries at this time. Courtesy of the Colonial Williamsburg Foundation, Virginia.

her innocence by cross-examining the elders who were subsequently stoned to death. Susannah was regarded as the ideal wife and Robert Aylett's book *Susanna or the Arraignment of the Two Unjust Elders* published in 1622 emphasised the importance of domestic skills.[24] Joseph fleeing from the seductive attentions of his master Potiphar's wife can be read as a male version of the story which Xanthe Brooke suggests may also represent the tenth commandment and she cites its widespread appearance in Dutch art and furnishings.[25]

In many of the biblical scenes figures from fashionable society, their clothes detailed with some care, act out the central roles or mingle with figures in more historic styles of dress. In some cases this self-confident combination of traditional elements from 16th-century engravings and unconventional biblical characters in contemporary dress can lead to problems in identifying the subject, particularly in the case of King Solomon receiving the Queen of Sheba. When the king bears a credible resemblance to Charles I the issue is further confused. In such circumstances it is tempting to believe that the subject is really irrelevant and that the designs would have been produced to appeal to the young women who would have enjoyed the fashionable details of the costume. Illustrated broadsheets probably provided the basic design for many of these embroideries. They were sold separately or in sets of four or six and advertisements were produced listing the various designs available. Many of these include stock characters such as the king and queen who appear in several different stories, the elderly, bearded chamberlain in long robes, and a figure in armour who often portrays Mordecai or the soldier about to cut in half the disputed child on the steps of Solomon's throne.

One of the most finely worked and detailed of the embroidered panels showing a standard arrangement of figures includes a king and queen with a chamberlain and a lady in waiting [pl. 70]. The men wear wide bucket-topped boots lined with lace boot hose which became fashionable in the mid 1630s. Their short doublets are slashed to reveal their fine linen shirts and the man on the left carries a broad feather-trimmed hat. The aim was the careless, slightly dishevelled look we associate with the Cavaliers, in contrast to the neat, sober dress of the Puritans which is seldom depicted in these embroideries. The women's dresses with tabbed bodice, two-tier sleeves decorated with rosettes of ribbon, gauntlet cuffs and wide collars of linen trimmed with lace all indicate the fashionable styles of the 1640s. The hairstyles, a very useful indicator of date, confirm this. This panel was illustrated in Marcus Huish's book published in 1900 to coincide with an exhibition at the Fine Art Society in London. It was entitled 'Charles I and his Queen' and dated 1630, although the clean-shaven king and the costume suggest a later date.

Comparison with another almost identical composition worked a few years later shows the change in fashion [pl. 71]. The most distinct differences are the more vertical line of the women's dress and the exaggerated length of the men's shoes in the later version. New or extreme fashions are always open to criticism and the 17th century was no exception. In the 1620s women were condemned for baring their forearms and during the 1630s for wearing looser gowns. Loose gowns were equated with loose morals. Men were not exempt. In *Anthropomorphosis: Man Transformed or the Artificial Changeling* (1650) John Bulwer criticised men for distorting their feet with long-toed shoes to the extent that they could hardly kneel in church and John Evelyn decried the wide ribbon-trimmed breeches as effeminate.[26] Indeed these breeches were known as petticoat breeches because of the amount of fabric used. However, attempts to reform and control dress during the austerity of the Common-

70. DETAIL OF PANEL, *c.* 1640S
The fashionable dress is carefully depicted. For example, the king wears bucket-topped boots which are lined
with lace boot hose and have red heels. His wide-legged breeches are trimmed with ribbons and his lace shirt cuffs
are turned back over the sleeves of his doublet. The queen's dress, including the elaborate lace collar,
is also precisely detailed. 33.5 cm × 43.5 cm (29/65).

wealth were unsuccessful. This was perhaps hardly surprising as some of the Puritans, including Cromwell's family, despite adopting a more restrained sober style in keeping with their ascetic attitudes, still dressed in expensive silks and the finest of linens.

Although costume details can be very useful in the dating of these pictures they are not an infallible guide. The unfinished sampler said to have been worked by Mary of Modena

(1658–1718), as she was known, shows a female figure wearing what appears to be fashionable dress of the late 1620s or early 30s, with a wired, standing collar edged with lace [pl. 40]. The figure may have been adapted from an earlier design of Galatea in Jacob Cats' *Silenius Alcibiadis, sive Proteus* published in 1618. As the figure on the sampler wears flowers in her hair and carries a rose she probably represents Flora or spring, or the sense of smell. However, if the costume is contemporary with the date of the needlework it could not have been worked by Mary of Modena.

There were times during the early years of the century when bare breasted styles were considered to be the height of fashion, but this can be misleading. Classical, allegorical and biblical figures are often shown in this style irrespective of date. Figures wearing classical, fashionable and an imaginative version of biblical dress are often combined in one story. Examples of such combinations can be seen in the Collection in two panels depicting David and Bathsheba [pls 73, 74] and one embroidery of Lot and his daughters with angels (29/51).

Unrelated elements are very often combined in an ingenious way. Mythological creatures such as harpies, cockatrice and unicorns appear with lions, stags and leopards in landscapes strewn with flowers as in *millefiori* tapestries. They crowd around the main action of the pictures with little concern shown for scale or perspective. However, they contribute to the overall decorative quality of the piece and repay careful scrutiny as they are full of unexpected humour and delightful detail. John Taylor's poem provides an excellent description of this diversity:

> Flowers, Plants and Fishes, Beasts, Birds, Flyes and Bees;
> Hills, Dales, Plaines, Skies, Seas, Rivers and Trees;
> There's nothing neere at hand, or furthest sought,
> But with the Needle may be shap'd and wrought.
> In clothes of Arras I have often seen,
> Men's figur'd counterfiets so like have been,
> That if the parties selfe had been in place,
> Yet Art would vye with Nature for the grace.
> Moreover, Posies rare, and Anagrams,
> Signifique searching sentences from names,
> True History, or various pleasant fiction,
> In sundry colours mixt, with Arts commixion,
> All in Dimension, Ovals, Squares, and Rounds,
> Arts life included within Natures Bounds:
> So that Art seemeth meerley naturall,
> In forming shapes so Geometricall.

The love of nature is obvious in all of these embroideries and reflects the 17th-century ideal of the pastoral paradise, represented by the mythological country of Arcadia, as a retreat

71. DETAIL OF PANEL SHOWING SOLOMON AND THE QUEEN OF SHEBA, *c.* 1650S

King Solomon receives gifts from the Queen of Sheba. The maid carrying the parasol is a stock figure who appears in various stories. The king, who bears a strong resemblance to Charles I, and the queen are decorated with beads and seed pearls. 38.5 cm × 49.5 cm (29/66).

Gerardus de Jode
excudebat

Dum lavat et recreat gelido sua flumine membra Bersabee regis litera missa datur. 2. Reg. cap. 11.

72. DAVID AND BATHSHEBA
Engraving from Gerard de Jode, *Thesaurus Sacrarum Historiarum Veteris Testamenti,* Antwerp 1585.
Courtesy of the Trustees of the National Library of Scotland.

from the life of the town and court. There was a profound change in the English landscape during the 17th century, brought about by the influence of Dutch refugees and the enclosure of common grazing land. This resulted in increased pastoralisation and more arable cultivation. The advances in agriculture were recognised by the new gentry and by merchants who invested in improvements in animal husbandry. In turn this new interest in agriculture is reflected in several embroidered scenes such as plate 77 which shows a rural idyll, with a shepherd playing a pipe, a fisherman, a woman milking a cow, a farmer ploughing, a huntsman in pursuit of deer, and, in the corner, an allegorical figure with a basket of fruit representing Nature or Plenty. These scenes have their origins in medieval tapestries and would have appealed to the contemporary taste for Arcadian landscapes seen at their best in the paintings of Claude and Poussin. The pastoral paradise is closely associated with the idea

73. PANEL SHOWING DAVID AND BATHSHEBA, MID 17TH CENTURY

This version tells the whole story. King David sees Bathsheba, the beautiful wife of Uriah the Hittite, as she is bathing. He sends for her and as a result of her visit to the palace she becomes pregnant. David arranges Uriah's death in battle and marries Bathsheba. They are punished by the death of their child and David is shown seeking penance. 30.5 cm × 43.2 cm (29/58).

74. PANEL DEPICTING DAVID AND BATHSHEBA, *c.* 1650–80

Padded and raised embroidery with canvas work stitches, silk and metal threads, covered purl and beads. David wears plush stitch garments and the butterfly's body is made from bits of straw. A whimsical touch is added to the scene by the large green spider which appears to have escaped from the border and crawls across the front of the palace building. 38 cm × 48 cm (29/59).

75. RUSTIC SCENE, POSSIBLY A PANEL FROM A CUSHION, EARLY 17TH CENTURY
Among the recognisable plants are a cowslip, a columbine, a thistle, pinks and peapods. On the reverse is a note stating: 'This piece of work was left to me by my great aunt, Louise Dacres. It had been for a very long time in their family and I believe came through the Dalrymples, her mother's family. She being the daughter of Sir Hew Dalrymple. Nina H Butler'. 32 cm × 50 cm (29/121).

76. (FACING) DETAIL FROM RUSTIC SCENE [PL.75]
Music was often depicted in 17th-century fine and decorative art. Folk, or country, music was danced to by all classes of society including the court, and was popular until the late 17th century. (29/121)

of the Golden Age, a time of innocence when man lived in harmony with his fellow man and with Nature. These idealised images [pls 76, 77] gradually superseded the Old Testament stories and are the origin of embroidered pastoral scenes with shepherds and shepherdesses which appear at the very end of the 17th century and the first half of the 18th century [pl. 78]. Many classical texts also eulogise the rural idyll, and as Latin was still the language of the educated in the 17th century, works such as Virgil's *Eclogues* and *Georgics* were widely read and became the source of many ideas for embroidered designs in the early 18th century.

77. PANEL SHOWING RURAL PURSUITS, MID 17TH CENTURY
Similar to the background subjects depicted in a set of four Sheldon tapestries representing the seasons which were derived from engravings by Martin de Vos. This panel may represent Spring. 39.5 cm × 51 cm (29/89).

78. PANEL DEPICTING A SHEPHERD AND SHEPHERDESS, *c.* 1700
Similar figures were used on all kinds of furnishings throughout the 18th century. Formerly in the collection of
Mrs Rachael Head. 26.5 cm × 30 cm (29/91).

79. BACK OF A CASKET, *c.* 1650–1700

Worked in silk threads on paper or vellum, this technique is known as colifichet. The panel depicts the meeting of Isaac and Rebecca. 18 cm x 26 cm (29/169).

APPENDIX: EQUIPMENT

80. THIMBLE HOLDER, LATE 17TH CENTURY

The pocket on the bird's back is closed by means of the drawstring at the front. Three-dimensional embroideries such as this may have been made by young girls after the completion of their caskets. A similar, but smaller, bird is among the items made by Martha Edlin (born 1660) in the early 1670s. These are now in the Victoria and Albert Museum, London. Length 14 cm (29/172).

EQUIPMENT

THE EQUIPMENT needed to carry out embroidery was very simple and consisted of a frame on which to stretch the fabric to keep it taut, scissors or a knife, pins and needles. Scissors with crossed blades were the same as those used today and others such as clippers and folding pocket types were known. Thimbles of bone, engraved silver and other materials were used [pl. 80].

The various types of needle available were listed by Randle Holme of Chester, a 'Gentleman Sewer in Extraordinary' to Charles II and James II, who published his *Academy of Armoury* in 1688.

> Sorts of Needle. Pearl needle is the least size of needles. The first, second and third sorts of Needles, according to their sizes until you come to ten. Ordinary needles. Buth Lane needles. Glovers needles have square points. Book Binders needles are long and round points. Sow-gelders needles are flat pointed. Chyrurgions needles are the same, flat pointed. Pack needles, crooked at the point, and some flat; others three square; others with a Back and Edge (like a Knife) at point.

Needles were either of drawn wrought iron, which distorted and broke easily, or of steel. Good quality Spanish steel needles were hard and resilient and known as sprior needles. A comedy, *Gammer Gurton's Needle* published in 1566, tells the story of an old woman who loses her sprior needle, which throws the whole village into confusion because it is the only one in the village. This would not have been unusual among small rural communities where steel needles would have been highly prized.

Pins too were very necessary and made in various sizes for holding different pieces of clothing together when worn. They were carefully looked after, even among the better off, and bent and damaged ones would be returned to the pinner for straightening and sharpening. Occasionally pins appear in portraits along with other status symbols. A portrait of Elizabeth Vernon, Countess of Southampton, painted *c.* 1600 and now in Boughton House, shows her informally in the process of dressing, a well stocked pin-cushion on the table beside her jewellery.

Pins were made in two parts with the head soldered to the shank. As a man could make only twenty per day they were scarce and expensive. It is possible that the expression 'pin money' derives from the need for women to save up to buy them. In a successful effort to improve economic conditions paupers from the Bristol workhouses were employed to make pins early in the 17th century. Later Charles I renewed import restrictions to encourage the establishment of a local industry. Children who worked samplers and caskets were made well aware of the arduous and dangerous business of needle and pin making as they were often threatened with apprenticeship to the trade if they misbehaved. It is part of the mythology of needle making that Elizabeth Stuart, daughter of Charles I, who was imprisoned in Carisbrooke Castle, died after Cromwell's government threatened to apprentice her to the trade.

81. DETAIL OF THE SIDE OF A CASKET, *c.* 1650–80 [PL. 42]
The winged figure is worked in silks over a padded and wired shape. The construction can be seen where the silk covering of the hand has worn away. 13.5 cm x 17 cm (29/169).

82. SAMPLER,
MID 17TH CENTURY
[PL. 9]
Samplers worked with spot
motifs were useful references
for designs and techniques.
They may have been rolled
and stored in workboxes
with sewing equipment.
52.7 cm x 26 cm (31/6).

Within the image (inscribed panels):

Animalium quadrupedum, Auium, florum,
fructuum, Muscarum et Vermium Omnis
generis Verae delineationes in aes incisae.

ORPHEVS
Ar to be sould
by Thomas Iohnson
in Britaines
Burse
1630

A Booke of Beast, Birds, Flowers, Fruits,
Flies, and Wormes, exactly drawne with
their Liuely Colours truly Described

May Menzies

83. ORPHEUS CHARMING THE ANIMALS, 1630

The title page of Thomas Johnson's book of designs which belonged to May Menzies who became governess to
Grisell and Rachel Baillie in 1705. The book originally belonged to her grandmother Katherine Logan.
Property of the Earl of Haddington.

NOTES

OTHER COLLECTIONS

CHRONOLOGY

BIBLIOGRAPHY

INDEX

NOTES

1 Nichols, John, *The Progresses, Processions and Magnificent Festivities of King James the First,* Vol. III, 1828, p. 563.

2 Arnold, J, *Queen Elizabeth's Wardrobe Unlock'd,* Leeds 1988, pp. 189–92.

3 *State Papers, Domestic,* 1660, p. 191, quoted by John Nevinson in *Catalogue of English Domestic Embroidery,* London 1950, p. xiii.

4 *Ibid.*

5 *Ibid.*

6 Swain, M and Nevinson, J, *Bulletin of the Needle and Bobbin Club,* Nos 1 and 2, New York 1982.

7 Marshall, R K, 'The Plenishings of Hamilton Palace in the Seventeenth Century', *Review of Scottish Culture,* No. 3, 1987, p. 13.

8 Jesse's *Historical Memorials,* Vol. IV, p. 89, quoted by Seligman and Hughes in *Domestic Needlework,* London 1926, p. 89.

9 Quoted by C Willet and Phillis Cunnington in *Handbook of English Costume in the Seventeenth Century,* London 1972.

10 Nevinson, J, 'The Embroidery Patterns of Thomas Trevelyon', *Walpole Society,* Vol. 41, 1968.

11 Slater, M, *Family Life in the Seventeenth Century: The Verneys of Claydon House,* London 1984, p. 243.

12 Swain, M, 'The Mellerstain Panel', *Apollo,* July 1966, p. 62.

13 Mayhew, Charlotte E J, The Effects of Economic and Social Developments in the Seventeenth Century, upon British Amateur Embroideries, with particular reference to the Collection in the National Museums of Scotland', M. Litt. thesis, University of St Andrews 1988.

14 Hackenbroch, Y, *English and Other Needlework, Tapestries and Textiles in the Irwin Untermyer Collection,* London 1960, p. xxxix.

15 Brooke, Xanthe, *The Lady Lever Art Gallery Catalogue of Embroideries,* Merseyside 1992, p. 92.

16 Lopez, Nella y Samartini, Royo, *Fiori di Perle a Venezia,* Venice 1992, p. 25.

17 Brooke, *op. cit.,* p. 42.

18 *Ibid.,* p. 15.

19 Hibbert, Christopher, *Cavaliers and Roundheads: The English at War 1642–1649,* London 1993, title-page illustrated between pp. 274 and 275.

20 Fraser, A, *The Weaker Vessel: Women's lot in seventeenth century England,* London 1984, p. 163.

21 Swain, Margaret, *Historical Needlework: A Study of Influences in Scotland and Northern England,* London 1970, p. 47 and plates 24, 25.

22 Mayhew, *op. cit.*

23 Fraser, *op. cit.,* pp. 234–5.

24 Mayhew, *op. cit.*

25 Brooke, *op. cit.,* p. 21.

26 Ribeiro, Aileen, *Dress and Morality,* London 1986, p. 86.

OTHER COLLECTIONS

There are many 17th-century embroideries in country houses and museums.
The following are places where some important collections and individual pieces may be seen.

GREAT BRITAIN
Ashmolean Museum, Oxford
Blair Castle, Perthshire
Castle Museum and Art Gallery, Nottingham
Costume Museum, Bath
Embroiderers' Guild, Hampton Court Palace
Fitzwilliam Museum, Cambridge
Guildford Museum, Surrey
Hardwick Hall, Derbyshire
Holburne Museum and Craft Study Centre, Bath
Lady Lever Gallery, Liverpool
Mellerstain House, Berwickshire
Royal Museum of Scotland, Edinburgh
St Nicholas Kirk, Aberdeen

Traquair House, Peebles
Victoria and Albert Museum, London
Whitworth Art Gallery, Manchester

USA
Art Museum, Chicago
Cooper Hewitt Museum, The Smithsonian
    Institution's Museum of Design, New York
Metropolitan Museum of Art, New York
Museum of Fine Arts, Boston

CANADA
Museum of Fine Arts, Montreal
Royal Ontario Museum, Toronto

CHRONOLOGY

1603 Death of Elizabeth; accession of James VI and I

1605 Gunpowder Plot

1611 Authorised Version of the Bible published

1616 Death of William Shakespeare

1620 Pilgrim Fathers sail to America

1625 Death of James VI and I; accession of Charles I

1628 William Harvey publishes his discovery of the circulation of blood, laying the foundation of modern medicine

1629 Charles I dissolves Parliament

1632 Van Dyck enters royal service and settles in England

1634 Rubens completes Charles I's commission to paint the ceiling of the banqueting hall, Whitehall Palace

1638 Solemn League and Covenant signed by Scottish Calvinists

1642 Beginning of Civil War; Battle of Edgehill

1643 Parliament signs Solemn League and Covenant with the Scots; first meeting of the Westminster Assembly

1645 Introduction of the Self-Denying Ordinance and foundation of the New Model Army; Battle of Naseby

1646 Charles I surrenders to the Scots, end of first Civil War

1647 Charles I imprisoned at Carisbrooke Castle, Isle of Wight

1648 Start of second Civil War; Siege of Colchester; Battle of Preston; end of second Civil War

1649 Execution of Charles I; formation of the Commonwealth; poet John Milton appointed spokesman for the Commonwealth

1651 Battle of Worcester; escape of Charles II to France

1653 Dissolution of the Rump Parliament; Cromwell becomes Lord Protector and his army imposes severe Puritan rule

1658 Death of Cromwell

1660 Restoration of Charles II

1662 Marriage of Charles II and Catherine of Braganza; founding of Royal Society

1665 Great Plague kills 70,000 in London alone

1666 Fire of London

1673 Marriage of James, Duke of York, to Mary of Modena

1675 Greenwich Observatory completed and first Astronomer Royal, John Flamstead, appointed; Christopher Wren begins work on plan for the new St Paul's cathedral

1676 John Bunyan begins *Pilgrim's Progress* in Bedford county gaol

1677 Marriage of Princess Mary, daughter of James, Duke of York, later James II, to William of Orange

1685 Death of Charles II; accession of James II; Monmouth Rebellion; publication of Isaac Newton's *Mathematical Principles of Natural Philosophy* which forms the basis of all modern astronomy and physics

1687 James II dismisses Parliament

1688 James II deposed; arrival of William and Mary

1689 Accession of William and Mary; Henry Purcell writes the first English opera, *Dido and Aeneas*

1701 Act of Settlement

1702 Death of William III; accession of Queen Anne

BIBLIOGRAPHY

BOOKS

Alciati, Andrea, *Emblematum Liber*, Augsburg 1531

Ammon, Jost, *Caesareae Maiestatis*, Frankfurt 1579

Arnold, Janet, *Queen Elizabeth's Wardrobe Unlock'd*, Leeds 1988

Ashelford, Jane, *Dress in the Age of Elizabeth I*, London 1988

Best, Muriel, *Stumpwork: Historical and Contemporary Raised Embroidery*, London 1987

Boler, James, *The Needle's Excellency*, London 1634

Brooke, Xanthe, *The Lady Lever Art Gallery Catalogue of Embroideries*, Merseyside 1992

Cats, Jacob, *Silenius Alcibiadis, sive Proteus*, Middelburg 1618

Clabburn, Pamela, *The Needleworker's Dictionary*, London 1976

Cumming, Valerie, *A Visual History of Costume: The Seventeenth Century*, London 1984

Cunnington, C Willet and Phillis, *Handbook of English Costume in the Seventeenth Century*, London 1972

Digby, George Wingfield, *Elizabethan Embroidery*, London 1963

Embroiderers' Guild, *Treasures from the Embroiderers' Guild Collection*, Newton Abbot 1991

Fraser, Antonia, *The Weaker Vessel: Women's lot in seventeenth-century England*, London 1984

Hackenbroch, Yvonne, *English and other Needlework, Tapestries and Textiles in the Irwin Untermyer Collection*, London 1960

Hibbert, Christopher, *Cavaliers and Roundheads: The English at War 1642–1649*, London 1993

Hind, Arthur, *Engraving in England in the Sixteenth and Seventeenth Centuries*, Vol. III, London 1964

Holme, Randle, *The Academy of Armoury*, London 1688

Huish, Marcus, *Samplers and Tapestry Embroideries*, London 1900 and 1913

Irwin, John and Brett, Katherine, *The Origins of Chintz*, London 1970

Jode, Gerard de, *Thesaurus Sacrarum Historiarum Veteris Testamenti*, Antwerp 1585

Johnson, Thomas, *A Booke of Beast, Birds, Flowers, Fruits, Flies and Wormes etc.*, London 1630

Jourdain, Margaret, *English Secular Embroidery*, London 1910

Kendrick, A F, *A Book of Old Embroidery*, Studio Special Number, London 1921

King, Donald and Levy, Santina, *Victoria and Albert Museum's Textile Collection: Embroidery in Britain from 1200–1750*, London 1993

Lipski, Louis L and Archer, Michael *Dated English Delftware – Tin-glazed Earthenware 1600–1800*, London 1984

Lopez, Nella y Sammartini, Royo, *Fiori di Perle a Venezia*, Venice 1992

Marks, Richard, *Burrell: Portrait of a Collector*, Glasgow, 1983

Mayhew, Charlotte E J, *The Effects of Economic and Social Development in the Seventeenth Century, upon British Amateur Embroideries, with Particular Reference to the Collections in the National Museums of Scotland*, M. Litt. thesis, University of St Andrews 1988

McKerrow, R B, *Title-page Borders used in England and Scotland*, London 1932

Morrall, Michael, *History and Description of Needlemaking*, Manchester 1865

Nevinson, John, *Catalogue of English Domestic Embroidery of the Sixteenth and Seventeenth Centuries*, Victoria and Albert Museum, London 1938 and 1950

Overton, John, *A New Book of all Sorts of Beasts: or a pleasant Way to teach Yeoung Children to Reade almost as soon as Speake*, London 1671.

Overton, John, *A New and Perfect Book of All Sorts of Beasts, Flowers, Fruits, Butterflies etc.*, London 1674

Parker, Rozsika, *The Subversive Stitch*, London 1984

Ribeiro, Aileen, *Dress and Morality*, London 1986

Rollin, John G, *Needlemaking*, Shire Album, no. 71, 1981

Schoonhouse, Flor, *Emblemata*, Amsterdam 1640s

Scott Thomson, Gladys, *Life in a Noble Household 1641–1700* (paperback), London 1965

Sebba, Anne, *Samplers: Five Centuries of a Gentle Craft*, London 1979

Seligman, G S, and Hughes, T, *Domestic Needlework*, Country Life, London 1926

Shorleyker, Richard, *A Schole-house for the Needle*, London 1624

Slater, M, *Family Life in the Seventeenth Century: The Verneys of Claydon House*, London 1984

Stent, Peter, *A New Booke of Flowers, Beasts, Birds, invented by J Dunstall*, London 1662

Swain, Margaret, *Historical Needlework: A Study of Influences in Scotland and Northern England*, London 1970

____, *The Needlework at Traquair*, 1984

____, *Scottish Embroidery*, London 1986

____, *Embroidered Stuart Pictures*, Shire Album, no. 246, 1990

Symonds, Mary, and Preece, Louisa, *Needlework Through the Ages*, London 1928

Synge, Lanto, *Antique Needlework*, Poole, Dorset 1982

____, *The Royal School of Needlework Book of Needlework and Embroidery*, London 1986

Thornton, Peter, *Seventeenth Century Interior Decoration in England, France and Holland*, London 1978

Tours, Jean de, *The True and Lyvely Historyke Purtreatures of the Vvoll Bible*, Lyons 1553

Whitney, E Geoffrey, *A Choice of Emblems and other devices*, Leyden 1586

ARTICLES

Ashton, Leigh, 'Martha Edlin, A Stuart Embroideress', *Connoisseur*, Vol. LXXXI, 1925, pp. 215–23

Cabot, Nancy Graves, 'Pattern Sources of Scriptural Subjects on Tudor and Stuart Embroideries', *Bulletin of the Needle and Bobbin Club*, Vol. 30, New York 1946

Davenport, Cyril, 'Embroidered Bindings of Bibles in the Possession of the British and Foreign Bible Society', *Burlington Magazine*, Vol. IV, 1904, pp. 267–80

Harris, Jennifer, 'Hannah Smith's Embroidered Casket', *The Antique Collector*, July 1980, pp. 50–5

Head, Mrs, 'A Collection of Needlework Pictures', *Connoisseur*, Vol. I, 1901, pp. 154–61

____, 'English Secular Embroidery of the Sixteenth and Seventeenth Centuries', *Burlington Magazine*, Vol. IV, 1904, pp. 168–74

Hogarth, Sylvia D, 'The Stapleton-Wyvill Marriage Purse', *Textile History*, No. 20, 1989, pp. 21–32

Kendrick, A F, 'Embroideries at the Whitworth Gallery, Manchester', *Connoisseur*, Vol. LXXXVI, 1930, pp. 283–94

____, 'Embroideries in the Collection of Sir Frederick Richmond Bart', *Connoisseur*, Vol. XCV, 1935, pp. 282–9

Marshall, R K, 'The Plenishings of Hamilton Palace in the Seventeenth Century', *Review of Scottish Culture*, No. 3, 1987

Morris, Miss A F, 'Needlework Pictures: their Pedigree and Place in Art', *Connoisseur*, 1906, pp. 93–100

Morris, Frances, 'English Domestic Needlework at the Metropolitan Museum of Art', *Bulletin of the Needle and Bobbin Club*, Vol. 30, 1946, pp. 27–53

Nevinson, John L, 'Men's Costume in the Isham Collection', *Connoisseur*, Vol. XCIV, 1934, pp. 313–20

____, 'Peter Stent and John Overton, Publishers of Embroidery Designs', *Apollo*, Vol. XXIV, 1936, pp. 279–83

____, 'English Embroidered Costume, Elizabeth and James', *Connoisseur*, Vol. XCVII, 1936, pp. 23–8, 140–4

____, 'Unrecorded Types of English Embroidery in the Collection of Lord Middleton', Pt I and II, *Connoisseur*, Vol. CIII, 1939, pp. 16–20, 136–41

____, 'The Embroidery Patterns of Thomas Trevelyon', *Walpole Society*, Vol. 41, 1968, pp. 1–38

Ribeiro, Aileen, 'A Paradise of Flowers, Flowers in English Dress in the Late Sixteenth and Early Seventeenth Centuries', *Connoisseur*, June 1979, pp. 110–18

Swain, Margaret, 'Embroidered Pictures from Engraved Sources', *Apollo*, Feb. 1977, pp. 121–3

____, 'Engravings and Needlework in the Sixteenth Century', *Burlington Magazine*, Vol. 118, May 1977, pp. 343–4

____, and Nevinson, John, 'John Nelham, Embroiderer', *Bulletin of the Needle and Bobbin Club*, Vol. 65, New York 1982, pp. 3–19

Wace, A J B, 'An Exhibition of Old English Needlework, Hove', *Old Furniture*, Vol. II, 1927, pp. 112–22

____, 'Sheldon Tapestry Cushions in the Collection of Sir William Burrell', *Old Furniture*, Vol. IV, 1928, pp. 78–81

____, 'Antique Needlework in the Collection of Frank Ward', *Old Furniture*, Vol. IV, 1928, pp. 63–7

____, 'Embroideries from the Abingdon Collection', *Old Furniture*, Vol.V, 1928, pp. 39–45

____, 'English Embroideries Belonging to Sir John Carew Pole, Bart.', *Walpole Society*, Vol. XXI, 1932, pp. 43–65

____, 'Embroidery in the Collection of Sir Frederick Richmond, Bart.', *Apollo*, Vol. XVII–XVIII, 1933, pp. 207–12 and 23–8

____, 'English Domestic Embroidery, Elizabeth to Anne', *Bulletin of the Needle and Bobbin Club*, New York, Vol. XVII, 1935, pp. 12–37

EXHIBITION CATALOGUES

Ancient and Modern Embroidery and Needlecraft, Glasgow School of Art 1916

Old English Needlework of the Sixteenth and Seventeenth Centuries, Sidney Hand Ltd, London 1920

A Collection of Old English Needlework, Frank Partridge and Sons Ltd, London 1934

Rare Embroidery and Old Lace, Signet Library, Edinburgh 1948

British Embroidery Thirteenth to Nineteenth Century, Museum and Art Gallery, Birmingham 1959

Seventeenth Century Pictorial Needlework, Holburne of Menstrie Museum, Bath 1987

INDEX